THE BOOK OF

CHRISTMAS
FOODS

THE BOOK OF

CHRISTMAS FOODS

JANICE MURFITT

Photography by
PAUL GRATER

HPBooks
a division of
PRICE STERN SLOAN

ANOTHER BEST SELLING VOLUME FROM HPBOOKS

HPBooks
A division of Price Stern Sloan, Inc.
360 North La Cienega Boulevard
Los Angeles, California 90048
9 8 7 6 5 4 3

By arrangement with Salamander Books Ltd., and Merehurst Press, London.

This book was created by Merehurst Limited.
Ferry House, 51-57 Lacy Road, Putney, London SW15
Designer: Roger Daniels
Photography: Paul Grater
Home Economist Janice Murfitt
Color separation by Kentscan Limited
Printed in Belgium by Proost International Book Production

Library of Congress Cataloging-in-Publication Data

Murfitt, Janice
    The book of Christmas foods / by Janice Murfitt.
        p.   cm.
    Includes index.
    ISBN 0-89586-821-0
    1. Christmas cookery   I. Title.
TX739.2.C45M87   1989
641.5'68—dc20   89-31213
                                            CIP

CONTENTS

INTRODUCTION

This book is devoted entirely to Christmas, packed with exciting ideas and wonderful recipes and planned to make Christmas a joy, not a chore. Each section of the book has a mixture of recipes suitable for all occasions and all members of the family—some quick and easy to make, others more advanced creative recipes for special occasions.

Christmas Fare is the largest section, ranging from the old traditional favorite recipes—Christmas cakes, puddings, mince pies, roast turkey—as well as some delicious alternatives for those wishing to try something completely different. Recipes for fruits, wine, nuts and herbs made into tasty stuffings, vegetables presented in different ways, and pâtés and terrines suitable for a buffet party are given. Many recipes are for using leftover food to prepare quick and tempting dishes.

Other sections included in this book are canapés offering tiny mouthfuls of tempting food made from a variety of cheeses, meat, fish, eggs or vegetables—all so pretty and quick to make. These can be served with a variety of drinks made from the drinks section.

As separate sections, Desserts & Puddings and Cakes & Cookies have a good selection of simply delicious recipes, many of which may be made in advance or kept in the freezer until needed. Try using different fruits than those suggested in the recipes.

Gifts and Decorations are very special sections with recipes that take a little longer, but can be made in advance and stored for several weeks. The delicate sugar cards are a joy to make and to receive, or try making a festive bread ring, made in the design given in the recipe or make your own design to hang up with pretty ribbon or place on the table as a centerpiece. The chocolates and sweets look so pretty when packed in tiny boxes and tied with ribbon, and make such a delightful gift for anyone, as do whole fruits in liqueurs, Spiced Citrus Slices, Brandied Mincemeat or Satsuma & Pine Nut Conserve.

I do hope this book gives you pleasure in preparing your own gifts, decorations and Christmas fare.

— PLANNING CHRISTMAS FOOD —

Christmas is a most wonderful time of year when family and friends meet to celebrate this happy occasion. Everything seems to buzz with excitement as the festivities fill the air—and the time should be one of happiness and giving.

However, so often as Christmas approaches, panic surrounds us and thoughts of how to plan the food; what to cook; how much to make and so on . . . fill our minds. *The Book of Christmas Foods* is designed to help answer these questions and includes all kinds of recipes relating to the festive season from traditional Christmas fare, such as the dinner and accompaniments, to cakes, puddings and mince pies, plus delicious alternatives and much, much more.

You will find simple recipes to make and freeze ahead of time; delicious desserts and puddings to impress your family and guests and a range of eye-catching canapés to serve with drinks or to make in quantity for a party. There's also a wonderful selection of cakes and cookies which offers a range of lovely ideas, including some novelty ones for children. The drinks section too, is sure to be popular with everyone as it caters to children as well as adults. Children will love to mix their own drinks, especially when they have friends to visit. And, last but not least there's a delightful selection of decorations and gifts to make ahead of time—which are fun to do and are sure to bring you compliments!

The Book of Christmas Foods has over 100 delicious recipes—each and every one illustrated with colorful and informative step-by-step photographs to help guide you to success every time. Each recipe section has been planned to make Christmas much easier, simply by containing a selection of ideas to suit all occasions and help make Christmas a wonderful, happy occasion.

The festive holiday spreads over several days and even into the New Year, so careful planning is the essence of success. Think ahead and plan the food required for each day of the holiday. Take into account the foods which will be left over, such as poultry, vegetables and fruit and select recipes to utilize these ingredients in the best way. Spend some time cooking certain foods

for the freezer to be prepared for those unexpected arrivals. Make a fish and meat pâté and freeze whole, or cut in slices (to thaw more quickly): serve with a salad and crusty bread to make a delicious impromptu meal. Freeze a few puddings or gâteaux for impressive desserts. Frozen finger foods also make marvelous standbys and certainly take the pressure out of entertaining at short notice. These tempting 'bites' offer so much and produce a tasty selection of foods to serve with drinks.

Once you have planned the menus and decided how many visitors are expected, work out which recipes may be made in advance—either to freeze or store until required, such as Christmas cakes, puddings and mince pies. And, if you've time, even fit in a few edible decorations and home-made gifts which will keep to help ease the pressure later on. Make a detailed shopping list of food to be purchased in advance and also for last-minute shopping. And stock up on drinks and ingredients for nibbles several weeks before to avoid the last minute rush in the days leading up to Christmas.

Try to make Christmas Eve part of the celebrations instead of being up to the early hours of the morning stuffing the turkey! Why not enjoy yourself and allow some time to wrap your home-made gifts prettily with ribbons and sprigs of holly or mistletoe, using a color scheme of matching paper, ribbons and gift tags. Preserves, Brandied Mincemeat, fruits in liqueurs, pretty sweets and cookies look most attractive arranged in baskets or boxes or in dainty glass or china dishes. Perhaps buy a preserve jar or a pretty spoon or dish to accompany Satsuma & Pine Nut Conserve. Assorted cheeses make a nice last-minute gift and look especially good placed in a basket with butter and crackers and a pretty festive napkin. Cookies or Gingerbread Houses make perfect novelty gifts for children. A Mini Christmas Cake with a few mince pies would make a most welcome gift for someone living alone, or make a mini-basket of homemade goodies, such as pâté, preserves, cake, Christmas pudding and cookies.

Bacon Aigrettes

4 slices bacon
1 tablespoon chopped fresh parsley
1/2 teaspoon ground black pepper
1/2 teaspoon Dijon-style mustard
Oil for frying

Choux Pastry:
2/3 cup water
1/4 cup butter
1/2 cup all-purpose flour
2 eggs

Dip:
2/3 cup plain yogurt
1 tablespoon chopped chives
1 tablespoon mango chutney

Cook bacon until crisp and chop finely. In a bowl, mix together bacon, parsley, pepper and mustard.

To prepare pastry, in a saucepan, heat water and butter until melted. Bring to a boil, remove pan from heat and immediately add all flour, beating vigorously to form a paste. Return to heat for a few seconds, stirring until paste forms a ball. Add eggs 1 at a time, beating until paste is very smooth and glossy. Stir in bacon mixture until well blended.

Half-fill a deep saucepan with oil. Heat to 360F (180C), or test by dropping small pieces of paste into oil. If it sizzles on contact, oil is hot enough. Drop teaspoonfuls of mixture into hot oil. Fry 3 to 4 minutes, turning once, or until puffed and golden brown. Drain on paper towels. Arrange on a serving dish. To prepare dip, mix yogurt, chives and chutney in a bowl. Serve with Bacon Aigrettes. Makes 35 to 40 pieces.

Asparagus in Chicory Leaves

8 oz. asparagus spears, trimmed
3 heads chicory
1 (8-oz.) pkg. cream cheese
3 slices proscuitto or parma ham
Tangerine wedges and dill sprigs to garnish

Marinade:
1 tangerine
1/2 clove garlic, crushed
1/4 teaspoon salt
1/4 teaspoon ground black pepper
1/2 teaspoon Dijon-style mustard
2 teaspoons honey
1 tablespoon plus 1 teaspoon olive oil
2 teaspoons chopped fresh tarragon

Half-fill a shallow skillet with water; bring to a boil. Add asparagus and cook 3 to 4 minutes or until spears are tender. Drain and cool in a shallow dish.

To prepare marinade, using a zester, cut peel of tangerine into fine strips; squeeze juice into a bowl. Add garlic, salt, pepper, mustard, honey, oil and tarragon and beat with a wooden spoon until thoroughly blended. Pour over asparagus, cover and chill for at least 1 hour.

Separate chicory leaves and cut in 1-inch lengths. Spread a little cream cheese onto each leaf. Cut asparagus spears in 1-inch lengths; place a piece of asparagus onto each chicory leaf. Cut proscuitto or ham in thin strips and wrap a piece around each chicory leaf. Garnish with tangerine wedges and dill sprigs. Makes 48 pieces.

Curried Vegetable Envelopes

2 oz. puff pastry, thawed
1 egg, beaten
1 teaspoon cumin seeds
Lime twists and herb sprigs to garnish

Filling:
1 tablespoon butter
1 leek, finely chopped
1 clove garlic, crushed
1 teaspoon ground cumin
1 teaspoon garam marsala
2 teaspoons mango chutney
1/2 teaspoon finely grated lime peel
2 teaspoons lime juice
1/2 cup cooked diced potato

Preheat oven to 425F (220C). To prepare filling, melt butter in small saucepan. Add leek and garlic.

Cook quickly, stirring, 1 minute. Add cumin, garam marsala, chutney and lime peel and juice. Stir well. Cook gently 1 to 2 minutes. Add potatoes, mix well and cool. Roll out puff pastry very thinly to a 12" x 8" rectangle. Cut in 2-inch squares. Brush edge with beaten egg and place a little filling in center of each square.

Draw all corners to center and seal joins like a tiny envelope. Arrange on a baking sheet. Brush envelopes with egg to glaze and sprinkle with cumin seeds. Bake in oven 5 to 8 minutes or until well risen and golden brown. Garnish with lime twists and herb sprigs. Makes 24 pieces.

Oysters with Eggplant

1 cup diced eggplant
Salt
6 large slices white bread
1/4 cup butter
2 tablespoons snipped chives
2 teaspoons chopped fresh oregano
4 button mushrooms, finely chopped
1/2 teaspoon ground black pepper
2 teaspoons fromage frais
12 fresh oysters in shells
3/4 cup soft bread crumbs
Oregano sprigs to garnish

Place eggplant in a bowl. Sprinkle with salt. Cover and let stand 30 minutes.

Preheat oven to 425F (220C). Cut crusts off bread. Roll slices flat with a rolling pan. Cut in 24 (2-inch) rounds using a daisy cutter. Spread both sides with some butter and press into muffin pans. Bake in oven 5 minutes or until lightly browned.

Drain and rinse eggplant. Dry on paper towels. Melt remaining butter in a saucepan. Add eggplant, chives, chopped oregano, mushrooms, pepper and some salt. Fry quickly, stirring occasionally, until eggplant is tender. Stir in fromage frais. Scrub oyster shells. Open and remove oysters. Cut each in half and place a half into each bread cup. Top with eggplant mixture and sprinkle with bread crumbs. Return to oven 10 minutes or until bread crumbs are lightly browned. Garnish with oregano sprigs. Makes 24 pieces.

Oatie Brie Cubes

1-1/2 cups soft bread crumbs
1/4 cup regular oatmeal
1/2 teaspoon salt
1/2 teaspoon ground black pepper
1/2 teaspoon dry mustard
2 eggs
8 oz. firm Brie or Camembert cheese
Oil for frying
Bay leaves, cranberries and lime wedges to
    garnish

Dip:
3/4 cup cranberries
Grated peel and juice 1 lime
1 tablespoon superfine sugar

In a bowl, mix bread crumbs, oatmeal, salt, pepper and mustard. Beat eggs in a small bowl.

Cut cheese in bite-sized cubes. Place 1 cube at time into beaten eggs, then coat evenly in oatmeal mixture. Repeat to coat all cheese cubes. Repeat to coat cheese cubes a second time in eggs and oatmeal mixture. Chill until needed.

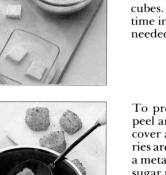

To prepare dip, place cranberries and lime peel and juice in a saucepan. Bring to a boil, cover and cook 1 to 2 minutes until cranberries are tender. In a food processor fitted with a metal blade, process cranberry mixture and sugar until smooth. Pour into a small serving dish. Half-fill a saucepan with oil. Heat to 350F (175C) or when a cheese cube sizzles immediately. Fry about 6 cheese cubes at a time until pale golden. Drain on paper towels. Garnish with bay leaves, cranberries and lime wedges. Serve with dip. Makes 20 pieces.

Crab & Fennel Puffs

1 recipe Choux Pastry, page 10
1 egg yolk, beaten
2 teaspoons sesame seeds
Fennel sprigs and radish slices to garnish
Cayenne pepper

Filling:
1 tablespoon butter
3 tablespoons finely chopped green onions
3 tablespoons finely chopped fennel
1/3 cup white crab meat
1/4 cup dark crab meat
1/2 teaspoon finely grated lemon peel
1/4 teaspoon ground black pepper
1 tablespoon sour cream
Cayenne pepper

Preheat oven to 425F (220C). Grease 2 baking sheets.

Place pastry in a piping bag fitted with a 1/2-inch plain nozzle. Pipe about 40 small rounds of pastry, spacing apart, onto greased baking sheets. Brush with egg yolk and sprinkle with sesame seeds. Bake in oven 15 to 20 minutes or until crisp and golden brown. Cool on a wire rack. To prepare filling, melt butter in a small saucepan. Add green onion and fennel. Cook 1 to 2 minutes or until tender. Remove pan from heat. Stir in light and dark crab meat, lemon peel, pepper and sour cream until well blended.

Cut each pastry ball across top. Fill each with crab filling and dust with cayenne pepper. Arrange on a serving plate. Garnish with fennel sprigs and radish slices. Makes 40 pieces.

Cheese Straws

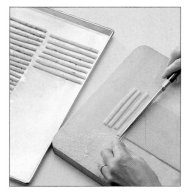

Cheese Pastry:
2 cups all-purpose flour
1/2 teaspoon salt
1/2 teaspoon cayenne pepper
1/2 teaspoon dry mustard
1/2 cup butter
1 cup shredded Cheddar cheese (4 oz.)
1 egg, beaten

Flavorings:
1 tablespoon plus 1 teaspoon finely chopped
    red and yellow bell peppers
1 clove garlic, crushed
1 tablespoon plus 1 teaspoon chopped fresh
    basil
1 tablespoon plus 1 teaspoon chopped fresh
    parsley
Red and yellow bell pepper twists and bay
    leaves to garnish

Preheat oven to 400F (205C). Grease several baking sheets. In a bowl, sift flour, salt, cayenne and mustard. Cut butter into pieces. Cut butter into flour mixture finely to resemble bread crumbs. Using a fork, stir in cheese and egg until mixture clings together. Knead to a smooth dough.

Cut pastry in 4 pieces. Flavor 1 piece with peppers, 1 with garlic, 1 with basil and remaining piece with parsley, kneading each piece lightly. Roll out 1 piece at a time to a 4-inch-wide strip that is 1/4-inch thick.

Using a knife, cut in 1/4-inch strips. Arrange in a straight line on greased baking sheets. Knead each of flavored trimmings together, re-roll and cut out rings using a 2-inch and 1-1/2-inch plain cutter. Place on baking sheets. Bake in oven 5 to 8 minutes or until golden. Cool on wire racks. Serve straws in bundles threaded through pastry rings. Garnish with bell pepper twists and bay leaves. Makes 100 pieces.

Crispy Pesto Shrimp

12 cooked peeled jumbo shrimp
6 large slices white bread
1/4 cup butter
1 clove garlic
1 tablespoon plus 1 teaspoon pesto sauce
1 teaspoon finely grated lemon peel
1/4 teaspoon salt
1/4 teaspoon ground black pepper
Lemon triangles and lemon balm leaves to
garnish

Cut each shrimp in half across width. Cut crusts off bread. Using a rolling pin, roll each slice flat.

In a small bowl, beat butter until soft and smooth. Stir in garlic, pesto sauce, lemon peel, salt and pepper. Beat until smooth and well blended. Spread both sides of each slice of bread with butter mixture and cut each slice in 4 triangles.

Place a shrimp in center of each bread triangle. Fold 2 points to center and secure with a wooden pick. Arrange on a grid in a grill pan and broil under a moderately hot grill until bread is lightly browned. Garnish with lemon triangles and lemon balm leaves and serve hot. Makes 24 pieces.

Festive Dip Selection

1 small eggplant
2 cloves garlic
1/2 cup sour cream
Salt
Ground black pepper
1 tablespoon chopped fresh rosemary
1 (8-oz.) pkg. cream cheese
2 tablespoons fromage frais
1/4 cup chopped fresh mixed herbs such as
    parsley, basil, thyme, oregano and chervil
2/3 cup red lentils
1-3/4 cups water
2/3 cup plain yogurt
Mixed vegetable sticks (zucchini, bell peppers,
    celery, cucumbers, carrots) baby sweet corn,
    cherry tomatoes and radishes

Preheat oven to 425F (220C) or use a hot grill.
Bake or grill eggplant until skin has charred
and flesh is tender, turning once. Cut eggplant in half, scoop out flesh, cool. Using a
food processor fitted with a metal blade, process eggplant, 1 clove of garlic, sour cream, salt
and pepper to taste and rosemary until mixture is smooth and creamy. Spoon into a serving bowl.

Place cream cheese, fromage frais, herbs and
salt and pepper to taste in a bowl. Beat until
soft and well blended. Spoon into a serving
dish.

In a saucepan, bring lentils and water to a
boil, then simmer gently until all water has
been absorbed. Cool. In food processor, process lentils, remaining garlic, salt, pepper and
yogurt until creamy and smooth. Spoon into a
serving dish. Serve dips with mixed vegetables. Each dip makes 6 to 8 servings.

Curry Whirls

1-1/4 cups all-purpose flour
1 teaspoon curry powder
1/2 teaspoon salt
1/2 teaspoon pepper
1/2 teaspoon dry mustard
1/2 cup butter
2 tablespoons Parmesan cheese
1 egg, beaten
1 teaspoon coriander seeds
Tomato wedges and parsley to garnish

Preheat oven to 425F(220C). Lightly grease several baking sheets. In a bowl, sift flour, curry powder, salt, pepper and mustard. Cut butter in pieces. Cut butter into flour mixture finely to resemble bread crumbs. Using a fork, stir in Parmesan cheese and egg until mixture clings together. Mix to a soft dough.

Place mixture in a pastry bag fitted with a star nozzle. Pipe about 40 swirls of mixture onto lightly greased baking sheets, spacing apart.

Sprinkle each swirl with coriander seeds and bake in oven 10 to 15 minutes or until lightly browned at edges. Cool on a wire rack. Arrange on a plate to serve. Garnish with tomato wedges and parsley. Makes 40 pieces.

Stuffed Leaves

10 small spinach leaves
10 small lettuce leaves
10 small radicchio leaves

Filling:
5 slices bacon
1 tablespoon plus 1 teaspoon chopped pickled
  vegetables
2 oz. Neufchâtel cheese
1/4 cup cooked white long-grain rice
1 teaspoon Dijon-style mustard
1/2 teaspoon salt
1/2 teaspoon ground black pepper
1 small red bell pepper, seeded
1 small yellow bell pepper, seeded

Bring a saucepan of water to a boil. Add spinach leaves. Bring back to boil, remove quickly and refresh leaves in cold water. Drain thoroughly and dry on paper towels. Repeat with remaining leaves. In a skillet, cook bacon until crisp. Chop bacon and pickled vegetables finely. Place Neufchâtel cheese in a bowl; beat until smooth. Add bacon, pickled vegetables, rice, mustard, salt and pepper. Stir until well blended.

Spread leaves out flat on a board. Place 1 teaspoonful of mixture on each leaf. Roll up and secure each with a wooden pick. Cut bell peppers in thin rings; cut rings in 4 pieces. Arrange stuffed leaves on a serving plate. Garnish with bell peppers. Makes 30 pieces.

Feta Cheese Kebabs

7 oz. feta cheese
1/4 red bell pepper
1/4 yellow bell pepper
1 zucchini
1/4 eggplant
Thyme sprigs and pink peppercorns

Marinade:
2 tablespoons olive oil
1 tablespoon raspberry vinegar
1 teaspoon honey
1/2 teaspoon Dijon-style mustard
2 teaspoons chopped fresh thyme
1/4 teaspoon salt
1/2 teaspoon ground black pepper

To prepare marinade, combine olive oil, vinegar, peppercorns, honey, mustard, thyme, salt and pepper in a large bowl with a wooden spoon until thoroughly blended. Cut feta cheese, bell peppers, zucchini and eggplant in bite-sized pieces. Add to marinade; stir well to coat evenly. Cover with plastic wrap and refrigerate at least 1 hour.

Thread 1 piece of each ingredient onto wooden picks. Just before serving, broil under a hot grill 2 to 3 minutes or until vegetables are just tender. Garnish with thyme sprigs and peppercorns. Makes 24 kebabs.

Chicken Liver Pouches

2 leaves phyllo or streudel pastry, thawed
1/4 cup butter, melted
1 teaspoon poppy seeds
Oregano sprigs and tomato wedges to garnish

Filling:
1 tablespoon butter
1 clove garlic, crushed
4 oz. chicken livers
1 tablespoon chopped fresh oregano
1/4 teaspoon salt
1/4 teaspoon ground black pepper
2 teaspoons all-purpose flour
2 teaspoons Marsala wine
2 tablespoons half and half

Preheat oven to 400F (205C). Line 2 baking sheets with parchment paper. To prepare filling, melt butter in a small saucepan. Add chicken livers and garlic and fry quickly 30 seconds. Stir in oregano, salt, pepper and flour until well blended. Add wine and half and half. Bring to a boil, stirring constantly. Remove from heat and cool.

Brush pastry sheets with melted butter; place one on top of the other. Using a sharp knife, cut pastry in 2-1/2-inch squares. Spoon a little filling onto each square. Draw up corners of pastry and press firmly together. Press down slightly to flatten. Brush each pouch with remaining butter and sprinkle with poppy seeds. Place pouches on prepared baking sheet. Bake in oven 5 minutes or until golden brown. Arrange on a warmed serving dish. Garnish with oregano sprigs and tomato wedges. Makes 24 pieces.

Cocktail Pinwheels

2-1/4 cups all-purpose flour
1/2 teaspoon salt
1/2 teaspoon cayenne pepper
1 teaspoon dry mustard
3/4 cup butter
1 cup shredded Cheddar cheese (4 oz.)
1 egg, beaten
Parsley sprigs to garnish

Flavorings:
1 teaspoon sesame seeds
1 teaspoon poppy seeds
1 teaspoon curry paste
2 teaspoons tomato paste

In a bowl, sift flour, salt, cayenne and mustard. Cut butter in pieces. Cut butter into flour mixture finely to resemble bread crumbs. Using a fork, stir in cheese and egg until mixture clings together. Knead in a smooth dough.

Cut pastry in 4 pieces. Knead sesame seeds into 1 piece and poppy seeds into another. Form both in 6-inch rolls. Wrap separately in plastic wrap. Roll remaining 2 pieces of pastry in 8" x 6" rectangles. Spread 1 piece with curry paste and other with tomato paste. Roll up each from long edge in 2 firm rolls. Wrap in plastic wrap. Chill until firm or freeze until needed.

Preheat oven to 400F (205C). Line several baking sheets with parchment paper. Cut each roll in thin slices and arrange a little apart on prepared baking sheets. Bake for 6 to 8 minutes or until golden. Cool, then transfer to wire racks. Garnish with parsley sprigs. Makes 96 pieces.

Lamb & Walnut Bites

8 oz. lamb fillet, cut up
1 cup soft bread crumbs
1 shallot
2 teaspoons fresh rosemary
1 teaspoon salt
1/2 teaspoon ground black pepper
1 egg
5 pickled walnuts
All-purpose flour
Rosemary sprigs to garnish

Sauce:
1 onion, finely chopped
1 clove garlic, crushed
3 large tomatoes, peeled, seeded, chopped
1 tablespoon chopped fresh basil
Oil for frying

In a food processor fitted with a metal blade, process lamb until finely chopped. Add bread crumbs, shallot, rosemary, salt, pepper and egg. Process until smooth. Cut pickled walnuts in small pieces. Using a little flour, press 1 teaspoonful of meat mixture in a flat round. Place a piece of walnut in center and form in a smooth ball. Repeat to make about 35 to 40 balls.

To prepare sauce, combine onion, garlic and tomatoes in a small saucepan. Bring to a boil and cook rapidly, stirring occasionally, until mixture is pulpy and thick. Stir in basil and pour into a serving dish. Half-fill a small pan with oil. Heat to 350F (175C) or to when a meat ball is placed in oil, it sizzles immediately. Fry meat balls in several batches 2 to 3 minutes or until lightly browned. Drain on paper towels. Serve with sauce. Garnish with rosemary sprigs. Makes 35 to 40 pieces.

Cheese Thins

1 cup all-purpose flour
1/2 teaspoon salt
1/2 teaspoon pepper
1/2 teaspoon dry mustard
1/2 cup butter
1 cup shredded Cheddar cheese (4 oz.)
1 tablespoon plus 1 teaspoon regular oats
1 teaspoon cayenne pepper
1 egg white
Fennel sprigs to garnish

Preheat oven to 425F (220C). Lightly grease 2 baking sheets. Sift flour, salt, pepper and mustard into a bowl. Cut butter into pieces. Cut butter into flour mixture finely until mixture begins to cling together.

Using a fork, stir in cheese and mix to a soft dough. Knead on a lightly floured surface and roll out very thinly. Using a 1-inch oval cutter, cut out 80 oval shapes. Arrange on greased baking sheets, spacing apart.

In a small bowl, mix oatmeal and cayenne. Brush each oval with egg white and sprinkle with oatmeal mixture. Bake in oven to 5 to 6 minutes or until pale in color. Cool on baking sheets a few minutes, then remove carefully with a palette knife. Arrange on a plate to serve. Garnish with fennel sprigs. Makes 80 pieces.

Herbed Crepe Pinwheels

1/2 cup all-purpose flour
1/4 teaspoon salt
1/4 teaspoon ground black pepper
1 egg
1/4 cup milk
1 tablespoon fresh chopped basil
Oil
Cherry tomato wedges and herb sprigs to
    garnish

Filling:
8 large spinach leaves
1/2 (8-oz.) pkg. cream cheese with herbs and
    garlic, softened
8 thin slices proscuitto or Parma ham

To prepare batter, sift flour, salt and pepper into a bowl. Mix in egg and 1/2 of milk with a wooden spoon; beat until smooth. Stir in remaining milk and basil. Beat until well blended.

Heat a little oil in a small skillet. Add 1 spoonful of batter; swirl pan to coat thinly. Cook until crepe is pale golden on both sides, turning only once. Place on paper towels. Repeat to make 8 crepes.

In a saucepan, cook spinach leaves 1 minute in boiling salted water. Drain and cool. Cover 1 crepe with a spinach leaf, spread with some cream cheese and cover with a slice of proscuitto or Parma ham. Roll up firmly and wrap in plastic wrap. Repeat to make 8 crepe rolls. Just before serving, cut each roll in 1/2-inch slices. Arrange on a serving plate. Garnish with cherry tomato wedges and herb sprigs. Makes 48 pinwheels.

Party Quiches

1/2 cup all-purpose flour
1/4 teaspoon salt
2 teaspoons butter
2 to 3 teaspoons cold water
Red bell pepper rings and fennel sprigs to
    garnish

Filling:
1 egg
2 tablespoons half and half
1/4 teaspoon salt
1/4 teaspoon pepper
1/4 teaspoon dry mustard
2 teaspoons finely chopped bell peppers,
2 teaspoons chopped button mushrooms
2 teaspoons chopped crispy bacon
2 teaspoons chopped fresh herbs

Sift flour and salt into a bowl. Cut butter in
pieces. Cut butter into flour mixture finely
until mixture resembles bread crumbs. Using
a fork, stir in water until mixture begins to
bind together. Knead to a firm dough.

Roll out pastry thinly on a lightly floured surface. Line 24 tiny pastry boat molds or tiny
round tart pans with pastry. Prick pastry and
chill 1 hour. Preheat oven to 425F (220C).
Bake pastry molds in oven 5 minutes, then
remove from oven.

To prepare filling, place egg, half and half,
salt, pepper and mustard into a bowl. Whisk
until well blended. Half-fill each pastry with
egg mixture, then fill with chopped bell peppers, mushrooms, bacon and herbs. Return to
oven 5 to 6 minutes or until filling has set.
Cool slightly, then slip pastry out of molds.
Serve warm or cold. Garnish with bell pepper
rings and fennel sprigs. Makes 24 pieces.

Mussels with Tomato Sauce

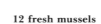

12 fresh mussels
2 tablespoons butter
2 tomatoes, peeled, seeded, chopped
2 tablespoons chopped chives
2 tablespoons chopped fresh basil
1 clove garlic, crushed
1 tablespoon tomato paste
1/4 teaspoon salt
1/4 teaspoon ground black pepper
1/2 teaspoon sugar
6 slices brown bread
2 tablespoons vegetable oil
3 pitted prunes, cut in pieces, and basil leaves
    to garnish

Scrub mussels and remove beards. Place in a saucepan, cover and heat gently until shells have opened. Cool and discard any mussels that do not open. To prepare sauce, melt butter in a saucepan. Stir in tomatoes, chives, basil, garlic, tomato paste, salt, pepper and sugar. Bring to a boil, stirring occasionally. Cook gently 2 minutes or until thick.

Cut bread in 24 daisy shapes using a 1-inch daisy cutter. Heat oil in a skillet. Fry bread shapes until golden brown. Drain on paper towels. Remove mussels from shells; cut each in half and place on bread shapes. Top each with a spoonful of tomato filling and garnish with pieces of prune and basil leaves. Makes 24 pieces.

Creamy Filled Quail Eggs

12 quail eggs
4 large slices whole-wheat toast
1 tablespoon butter
2 teaspoons red lumpfish caviar and dill sprigs
   to garnish

Filling:
1/3 cup cooked garbanzo beans
2 tablespoons whipping cream
1/2 teaspoon salt
1/2 teaspoon ground black pepper
1 teaspoon Dijon-style mustard

Bring a small saucepan of water to a boil. Add quail eggs and cook 3 minutes. Drain and cover with cold water. Peel and cut in halves. Scoop out yolks.

To prepare filling, in a food processor fitted with a metal blade, process garbanzo beans until smooth. Add egg yolks, whipping cream, salt, pepper and mustard and process until smooth and creamy. Place filling in a pastry bag fitted with a small star nozzle. Pipe swirls of mixture into egg whites.

Cut toast in tiny ovals or rounds using a 1-inch cutter. Spread thinly with butter and sit a filled egg on each. Garnish with a little lumpfish caviar and dill sprigs. Makes 24 pieces.

Crispy Bacon Pinwheels

3/4 cup shredded Cheddar cheese (3 oz.)
1/4 teaspoon salt
1/4 teaspoon pepper
1/2 teaspoon Dijon-style mustard
2 tablespoons plain yogurt
6 large slices white bread
3 tablespoons butter
6 slices bacon
Celery leaves and radish slices to garnish

In a bowl, mix cheese, salt, pepper, mustard and yogurt. Cut crusts off bread; roll slices flat with a rolling pin. Spread each slice with butter and invert. Spread unbuttered sides evenly with cheese mixture and roll each up in a firm roll.

Stretch each bacon slice with a knife and cut in 3 pieces. Cut each bread roll in 3 rolls and wrap a piece of bacon around each roll. Secure with a wooden pick. Cover with plastic wrap and chill until needed.

Just before serving, broil bacon rolls under a hot grill until bacon is crisp and golden brown. Cool slightly, remove wooden picks and cut each roll in 3 slices. Garnish with celery and radish slices. Makes 54 pinwheels.

— Marinated Mushrooms with Grapefruit —

1 large pink grapefruit
1/3 cup ginger wine
2 teaspoons mint jelly
1/2 teaspoon salt
1/2 teaspoon ground black pepper
1 teaspoon Dijon-style mustard
48 button mushrooms
Mint leaves to garnish

Using a sharp knife, cut away grapefruit peel including white pith from flesh, allowing juice to fall into a small saucepan. Cut out segments in between membranes and place on a plate. Squeeze remaining juice from membranes into saucepan.

Stir in ginger wine, mint jelly, salt, pepper and mustard. Bring to a boil. Stir in mushrooms. Pour into a bowl and refrigerate until cold.

Cut grapefruit segments in bite-sized pieces. Reserve several grapefruit pieces for garnish. Thread mushrooms and grapefruit onto 24 wooden picks. Garnish with mint leaves and reserved grapefruit pieces. Makes 24 pieces.

Avocado Salmon Rolls

3 oz. smoked salmon slices
3 slices rye bread
1 tablespoon butter
Lemon twists and dill sprigs to garnish

Filling:
2 oz. cream cheese
1/2 avocado, mashed
2 teaspoons chopped fresh dill
1 small tomato, peeled, seeded, chopped
1/4 teaspoon ground black pepper

To prepare filling, beat cream cheese in a bowl until soft. Stir avocado into cream cheese until evenly blended. Add dill, chopped tomato and pepper and stir gently. Place in a pastry bag fitted with a 1/2-inch plain nozzle.

Cut smoked salmon in 20 (1-1/2" x 1") rectangles. Pipe a length of cheese mixture across top of short edge of each salmon rectangle and roll up.

Spread rye bread with butter. Cut in 20 rectangles to fit salmon rolls. Place salmon rolls on each piece of bread. Garnish with lemon twists and dill sprigs. Makes 20 pieces.

Filled Button Rarebit

1 cup soft white bread crumbs
1/4 cup chopped ham
1 tablespoon chopped fresh parsley
1 tablespoon fromage frais
24 button mushrooms
4 large slices white bread
2 tablespoons margarine
Celery leaves and parsley to garnish

Topping:
1 tablespoon cider
3/4 cup shredded Cheddar cheese (3 oz.)
1 teaspoon Worcestershire sauce
1/4 teaspoon salt
1/4 teaspoon ground black pepper
1/4 teaspoon dry mustard

Preheat oven to 425F (220C). To prepare filling, mix bread crumbs, ham, parsley and fromage frais in a bowl. Remove stalks from mushrooms, chop finely and stir into filling. Press filling into center of each mushroom. Cut out 24 rounds of bread to match size of mushrooms using a plain cutter. Spread both sides with margarine and place a mushroom on top of each bread round. Arrange on a baking sheet. Bake in oven 5 minutes, then remove.

To prepare topping, place cider in a saucepan. Bring to a boil. Remove saucepan from heat and stir in cheese, Worcestershire sauce, salt, pepper and mustard. Beat well. Spoon a little cheese mixture over top of each filled mushroom. Return to oven and bake 3 to 4 minutes or until cheese has melted and browned slightly. Arrange on a serving dish. Garnish with celery leaves and parsley. Makes 24 pieces.

Fondant Sweets

8 oz. ready-to-roll fondant icing (sugar paste)
Pink, green, yellow, violet and orange food
  colorings

Flavorings:
3 pieces marrons glacés
3 pieces crystallized ginger
1/2 teaspoon peppermint oil
1 teaspoon finely grated orange peel
1 teaspoon finely grated lemon peel
1 teaspoon finely grated lime peel

Cut fondant in 6 pieces. Tint 5 pieces very
pale pink, green, yellow, violet and orange.

Cut 2 marrons glacés and pink fondant in 8
pieces. Wrap each piece of marron glacé in
pink fondant and shape in a smooth ball. Repeat with violet fondant and crystallized ginger to make oval shaped sweets. Decorate
tops with remaining marron glacé and crystallized ginger.

Flavor white fondant with a few drops of peppermint oil. Roll out to 1/4-inch thickness.
Using a small round or crescent cutter, cut
out about 8 to 10 shapes. Knead orange peel
into orange fondant, lemon peel into yellow
fondant and lime peel into green fondant.
Shape each piece in tiny pinwheels, squares
or diamond shapes. Place all fondants on a
parchment paper-lined baking sheet to dry
out completely. Makes 40 pieces.

Hand-Dipped Chocolates

3 oz. ready-to-roll fondant icing (sugar paste)
Rose and violet flavorings
Pink and violet food colorings
2 oz. white marzipan
6 Brazil nuts
6 whole almonds
6 (1-oz.) squares semi-sweet chocolate
6 (1-oz.) squares white chocolate
6 (1-oz.) squares milk chocolate
6 maraschino cherries
6 creme de menthe cherries
Crystallized rose and violet petals

Cut fondant in 2 pieces. Flavor 1 piece rose and color pale pink with food coloring. Flavor remaining piece violet and color pale mauve with food coloring.

Roll out fondant to 1/2-inch thickness. Cut in shapes using cocktail cutters. Place on a waxed paper-lined baking sheet. Shape marzipan in various shapes by rolling bite-sized pieces between hands in balls, logs or ovals. Arrange on a baking sheet. Let dry several hours or overnight. Toast nuts until golden brown.

Melt each chocolate in different bowls over hand-hot water, stirring until melted. Using a fork, dip 1 center at a time into chocolate. Tap to remove excess and place chocolate on parchment paper-lined baking sheets. Leave plain, mark top with a fork or decorate rose and violet centers with crystallized petals. Continue to dip all centers, using white, dark or milk chocolate. Using a pastry bag, pipe some chocolates with threads of chocolate. Makes 30 pieces.

Chocolate Truffle Cups

16 (1-oz.) squares white chocolate
1/4 cup unsalted butter, melted
2 tablespoons whipping cream
1 tablespoon plus 1 teaspoon cherry brandy
1 tablespoon plus 1 teaspoon Chartreuse
    liqueur
1 tablespoon plus 1 teaspoon apricot brandy
Pink, green and yellow food colorings
6 pistachio nuts, chopped

Break up chocolate and place in a bowl set over a saucepan of hand-hot water. Stir occasionally until melted. Remove bowl from saucepan and cool. Place 36 foil cups on a tray. Spoon a little chocolate into each.

Using a fine brush, coat inside of each cup and refrigerate to set. Add melted butter and cream to remaining chocolate and stir until smooth. Divide mixture evenly among 3 bowls. Flavor 1 with cherry brandy and tint pink with food coloring; stir until well blended. Repeat to flavor and color 1 chocolate with Chartreuse and green food coloring and remaining chocolate with apricot brandy and yellow and pink food coloring.

When chocolate mixtures are set enough to peak softly, place each into a pastry bag fitted with a small star nozzle. Pipe swirls of each flavored chocolate into 12 chocolate cups. Sprinkle with pistachio nuts and let set. Pack into pretty boxes, baskets or dishes and cover with pretty paper and ribbon. Makes 36 pieces.

Kumquats in Cognac

1 lb. kumquats
1-1/4 cups water
1-1/2 cups sugar
2/3 cup cognac

Sterilize 2 or 3 small glass jars and lids and keep warm. Remove stalks and wash kumquats thoroughly. Dry on paper towels. Place water in a medium-sized saucepan. Add 1/2 cup sugar and heat gently, stirring occasionally, until sugar has dissolved. Bring to a boil.

Add kumquats and cook very gently 3 to 4 minutes, taking care kumquats do not split open. Remove kumquats with a slotted spoon and place on a plate. Place kumquats carefully in warm jars, without packing them too tightly, to neck of jar. Measure 2/3 cup of remaining syrup. Place in saucepan with remaining sugar. Stir over a gentle heat until sugar has dissolved.

Boil rapidly 1 minute until syrupy. Test by placing a drop of syrup between 2 cold teaspoons. Press together, then pull apart—a fine thread of sugar should form. Pour sugar syrup into a measuring cup and add same amount of cognac. Stir well and fill each jar to brim with cognac syrup. Seal jars with lids, label and store in a cool place up to 1 month. Makes 2 to 3 jars.

Spiced Citrus Slices

3 thin-skinned oranges
4 thin-skinned lemons
5 limes
Water
2-1/2 cups white wine vinegar
4-1/2 cups sugar
2 (2-inch) cinnamon sticks
2 teaspoons whole cloves
6 blades mace

Scrub fruit thoroughly. Cut each fruit in 1/8-inch thick slices. Lay slices in a stainless steel or enamel saucepan and just cover with water. Bring to a boil, cover and cook very gently about 10 minutes or until peel is tender. Drain slices and reserve liquor.

In another saucepan, gently heat vinegar, sugar and spices, stirring occasionally, until sugar has dissolved. Bring to a boil. Lay fruit slices in syrup. Add reserved liquor to cover fruit, if necessary, and cook very gently 15 minutes or until peel looks transparent.

Meanwhile, sterilize 3 small jars and lids. Arrange fruit slices in warm jars, alternating slices or packing each separately. Bring syrup to a boil. Immediately fill each jar to top and seal with lids. When cold, label and store in a cool place. Makes 3 small jars.

Lychees & Cherries in Chartreuse

10 fresh lychees or 1 (15-oz.) can lychees
2 cups fresh sweet cherries or 1 (15-oz.) can cherries
1 cup sugar
1-1/4 cups Chartreuse or Benedectine liqueur

Sterilize 3 or 4 small jars and lids and keep warm. Peel lychees and carefully remove pits, keeping fruit whole. Remove cherry stalks and pits. Wash cherries or drain canned fruit and dry on paper towels. Pierce skins of cherries all over with a clean needle or fine skewer.

Arrange 1 layer of cherries in 1 warm jar and sprinkle with a layer of sugar. Arrange 1 layer of lychees on top and sprinkle with more sugar. Continue to layer cherries, sugar and lychees until jar is loosely filled to neck of jar. Do not pack fruit tightly. Sprinkle with a final layer of sugar.

Fill jar to top with liqueur and seal with a clean lid. Repeat to fill more small jars with remaining fruit, sugar and liqueur. Store in a cool dry place up to 6 months. Makes 3 or 4 small jars.

—— Satsuma & Pine Nut Conserve ——

9 satsumas (2 lb. total)
About 2-1/2 cups water
4 cups sugar
1/4 cup orange flower water
1/2 cup pine nuts

Scrub satsumas well. Using a potato peeler or sharp knife, pare peel from satsumas, not including white pith. Cut peel in fine strips. Place in a large saucepan with 2/3 cup of water. Bring to a boil, cover and cook gently 1 hour or until tender.

Cut satsumas in half. Squeeze juice into a 2-cup glass measure. Add enough water to make 1-3/4 cups, if necessary. Reserve all seeds and place in a piece of muslin; tie securely with a string. Place in a saucepan with satsuma peel. Bring to a boil. Cover and simmer 1 hour. Strain liquid from satsuma peel into saucepan with peel. Stir in sugar and juice. Bring to a boil, stirring constantly, until sugar has dissolved.

Boil rapidly 5 to 10 minutes until setting point is reached. To test, spoon some conserve onto a cold plate. Let stand a few minutes, then push with your finger. If surface wrinkles, setting point has been reached. Add orange flower water and pine nuts. Bring to a boil and boil 2 minutes. Cool 30 minutes. Meanwhile, sterilize 3 jars and lids. Stir conserve, then pour into warm jars. Cover each with paraffin and seal with lids. Store in a dry cool place. Makes 3 jars.

Brandied Mincemeat

6 cups raisins
3-1/3 cups currants
1 cup dried apricots
3/4 cup dates
1 cup candied peel
3/4 cup whole almonds
1 lb. cooking apples, peeled, cored
Finely grated peel and juice 2 lemons
2-1/4 cups light-brown sugar
1 cup unsalted butter, melted
1 tablespoon ground mixed spice
2/3 cup brandy

In a large bowl, place raisins and currants. Chop or mince apricots, dates, candied peel, almonds and apples. Add chopped fruit and nuts and lemon peel and juice to raisins and currants. Mix well. Stir in brown sugar, butter, mixed spice and brandy.

Stir mixture until evenly blended. Cover with plastic wrap and refrigerate 2 days.

Sterilize 6 (1-pint) jars and lids and keep warm. Stir mincemeat thoroughly, then spoon into hot jars, filling each to top. Cover each with paraffin and seal with lids. Makes 6 (1-pint) jars.

Roast Stuffed Turkey

1 (8-lb.) oven-ready turkey with giblets
2-1/2 cups water

Stuffing:
4-1/4 cups soft white bread crumbs
1 large onion, finely chopped
3 celery stalks, finely chopped
Finely grated peel and juice 1 lemon
8 plums, pitted, chopped
2/3 cup red wine
2 cups chestnut puree
1 tablespoon chopped fresh sage
1 tablespoon chopped fresh thyme
1 tablespoon chopped fresh oregano
Salt and pepper to taste
1 lb. bacon
1/2 cup all-purpose flour

Remove giblets from turkey. Place in a sauce-pan with water. Bring to boil, cover and simmer 1 hour. Strain stock into a bowl; reserve liver. To prepare stuffing, place bread crumbs, onion, celery, lemon peel and juice, plums and wine in a saucepan. Bring to a boil, stirring constantly, and cook 1 minute. In a food processor fitted with a metal blade, process turkey liver, chestnut puree and herbs until smooth. Season with salt and pepper. Add bread crumb mixture and process until evenly blended.

Place 1/3 of stuffing into neck end of turkey. Pull over flap of skin and secure under turkey with skewers or string. Fill cavity of turkey with remaining stuffing. Pull skin over nose and secure with skewers or string. Truss turkey with string, securing wings and legs closely to body, and place in a roasting pan.

Preheat oven to 375F (190C). Cover whole turkey with strips of bacon over breast bone, body, legs and wings to keep moist during cooking.

Bake turkey in oven 2 hours. Remove bacon and cover turkey and pan with thick foil. Return to oven another 1 to 1-1/2 hours or until turkey is tender and only clear juices run when pierced with a knife between legs of turkey. Let stand in pan 20 minutes before removing. Remove any skewers or trussing string and place on a warmed serving dish. Chop crispy bacon finely.

To prepare gravy, blend flour and some stock until smooth. Strain stock into a saucepan and stir in flour mixture. Bring to a boil, stirring until thickened. Cook 2 minutes. Taste and season with salt and pepper and pour into a gravy boat. Serve turkey with bread stuffing and chopped bacon. Makes 10 servings.

—— Apple & Pickled Walnut Stuffing ——

2 tablespoons butter
4 shallots, chopped
1 lb. cooking apples, grated
Finely grated peel and juice 1 lemon
2 cups soft white bread crumbs
2 tablespoons chopped fresh thyme
1/2 teaspoon salt
1/2 teaspoon ground black pepper
1/2 cup chopped walnuts
5 pickled walnuts, sliced
1 egg, beaten

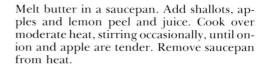

Melt butter in a saucepan. Add shallots, apples and lemon peel and juice. Cook over moderate heat, stirring occasionally, until onion and apple are tender. Remove saucepan from heat.

In a bowl, mix bread crumbs, thyme, salt, pepper and chopped and pickled walnuts.

Add apple mixture and beaten egg to bread crumb mixture. Stir well until evenly blended. Makes 5 cups.

Note
This recipe makes enough stuffing for a 5- to 6-lb. goose. Cut recipe in half for a duck or double recipe for a turkey.

Cranberry & Orange Stuffing

2 cups cranberries
Grated peel and juice 2 oranges
3 tablespoons honey
2 tablespoons butter
2 onions, chopped
1 teaspoon salt
1/2 teaspoon ground black pepper
1/2 teaspoon cayenne pepper
1 teaspoon ground mace
1 tablespoon plus 1 teaspoon chopped fresh
    sage
4-1/4 cups soft white bread crumbs
1/2 cup pine nuts

In a saucepan, combine cranberries and orange peel and juice. Bring to a boil. Cover and simmer very gently 1 minute or until cranberries are just tender. Remove saucepan from heat. Stir in honey. Pour cranberries into a bowl.

Melt butter in saucepan. Stir in onions and cook gently 2 minutes until tender. Add salt, pepper, cayenne, mace and sage and mix until well blended.

Stir onion mixture, bread crumbs and pine nuts into cranberries until well mixed. Makes 6 cups.

Note
This recipe makes enough stuffing for an 8-pound turkey. Cut recipe in half for a duck.

Gooseberry Goose

1 (8-lb.) oven-ready goose
2 tablespoons butter
6 shallots, finely chopped
6-1/4 cups soft bread crumbs
2/3 cup gooseberry juice
1-1/4 cups freshly chopped mixed herbs, such
    as marjoram, basil, thyme, rosemary, parsley
1 teaspoon salt
1 teaspoon ground black pepper
12 slices bacon
1 tablespoon Dijon-style mustard
1 cup elderflower wine
1 lb. gooseberries, cooked
1 tablespoon arrowroot
1 tablespoon plus 2 teaspoons superfine sugar
1/4 cup elderberries, if desired

Preheat oven to 425F (220C). Chop goose
giblets and reserve liver. Use giblets to prepare stock. Pierce skin of goose. To prepare
stuffing, melt butter. Add goose liver and
shallots and fry 2 minutes. Reserve 2 tablespoons of bread crumbs. Stir in 1/2 of
gooseberry juice, herbs, remaining bread
crumbs, salt and pepper until well mixed.
Stuff neck end and body cavity of goose. In a
roasting pan, cover goose with bacon and
bake 45 minutes. Reduce oven to 375F (190C)
and bake 1-1/2 hours, pouring off fat during
baking.

Chop bacon very finely. Mix bacon and
remaining bread crumbs. Brush goose with
mustard and sprinkle with bread crumb mixture. Bake another 20 to 30 minutes or until
meat is tender. Place on a serving plate. Pour
away fat. To prepare sauce, add 1/4 cup of
stock to roasting pan and mix with remaining
gooseberry juice, wine, gooseberries, arrowroot and sugar. Bring to a boil, stirring constantly and cook 1 minute. In a food processor, process sauce until smooth. Strain and
stir in elderberries, if desired. Serve sauce
with goose. Makes 8 servings.

Spiced Honey Ham

1 (3-lb.) smoked ham
Finely shredded peel and juice 2 oranges
2 tablespoons honey
1 teaspoon ground mace
1 teaspoon freshly grated ginger
4 oz. kumquats, sliced
2 tablespoons whole cloves
3/4 cup water
1 tablespoon cornstarch

Soak ham in a bowl of cold water overnight. Drain and transfer to a large saucepan. Cover with fresh cold water. Bring to a boil, cover and cook 30 minutes. Drain and cool. Remove skin from ham, leaving a layer of fat on surface of ham. Score fat in a lattice pattern with a sharp knife.

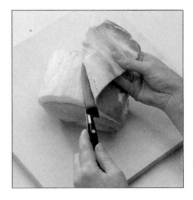

Preheat oven to 375F (190C). Place ham in a roasting pan. In a bowl, mix orange peel and juice, honey, mace and ginger until evenly blended. Brush surface of ham and bake in oven 30 minutes. Remove ham from oven and brush surface with more orange mixture.

Stud surface of ham with kumquat slices; hold in position with whole cloves. Return to oven another 30 to 40 minutes or until ham is golden brown and tender. Remove and place on a serving dish. Keep warm. To prepare sauce, add water to roasting pan. Stir to mix juices, then strain into a saucepan. Blend cornstarch with remaining orange juice and honey mixture. Add to pan, bring to a boil and cook 1 minute. Serve ham with sauce. Makes 8 servings.

Party Terrine

1 lb. pork, boned
1 lb. bacon
4 (4-oz.) boneless chicken breast fillets
1 lb. boneless veal
2/3 cup white wine
2 tablespoons Madeira wine
2 tablespoons chicken stock
2 teaspoons salt
1-1/2 teaspoons ground black pepper
10 juniper berries, crushed
2 cloves garlic, crushed
6 bay leaves
Additional bay leaves, orange twists and
    cranberries to garnish
Toast triangles, if desired

Preheat oven to 300F (150C). Using a mincer fitted with a fine blade or a food processor fitted with a metal blade, mince pork, bacon, chicken and veal. In a large bowl, combine meats, wines, chicken stock, salt, pepper, juniper berries and garlic. Mix together until thoroughly blended. Spoon mixture into a 7-1/2-cup ovenproof dish.

Press down firmly and arrange 6 bay leaves on top. Cover dish with a double thickness of foil. Stand dish in a pan half-filled with cold water. Bake in oven 1-3/4 to 2 hours or until terrine feels firm in center and shrinks from side of dish. Let stand until completely cold in dish. Garnish with additional bay leaves, orange twists and cranberries. Serve with toast triangles, if desired. Makes 20 servings.

Game Hens Noel

2 large game hens
4 slices bacon
1 tablespoon all-purpose flour
2/3 cup white wine
Chicken stock

Stuffing:
1 tablespoon butter
1 shallot, finely chopped
8 dried apricots, chopped
2 tablespoons corn kernels
1 tablespoon fresh chopped mixed sage, thyme
    and parsley
1/4 cup white wine
1/2 teaspoon salt
1/2 teaspoon ground black pepper

Preheat oven to 375F (190C). Place game hens into a small roasting pan. To prepare stuffing, melt butter in a saucepan. Add shallot and cook until tender, stirring occasionally. Remove saucepan from heat. Stir in apricots, corn, herbs, wine, salt and pepper. Stir until evenly mixed. Stuff game hens with stuffing; place in a roasting pan.

Cover breasts and bodies of game hens with strips of bacon. Bake 1 hour or until meat is tender. Remove bacon, chop finely and sprinkle over each game hen. Stir flour into juices in roasting pan and add wine. Bring to a boil, stirring constantly. Add some stock, if necessary, to dilute gravy. Cook 2 minutes. Serve sauce on game hens. Makes 2 servings.

Turkey Vegetable Strudel

9 leaves phyllo or strudel pastry, thawed
1/2 cup plus 3 tablespoons butter
1/4 cup all-purpose flour
1 bay leaf
1 cup milk
2/3 cup half and half
1/2 teaspoon salt
1/2 teaspoon ground black pepper
3/4 cup sliced leek
3/4 cup thinly sliced fennel
1 cup sliced button mushrooms
2/3 cup corn kernels
1 tablespoon plus 1 teaspoon chopped fresh
    parsley
1 cup diced cooked turkey

Cover phyllo pastry with a damp cloth to prevent drying. To prepare filling, combine 3 tablespoons of butter, flour, bay leaf and milk in a saucepan. Bring to a boil, whisking until thick. Cook gently 2 minutes. Stir in half and half, salt and pepper. Place 2 tablespoons of butter in a large skillet. Fry leek, fennel and mushrooms gently 2 to 3 minutes or until tender. Stir in corn, parsley and turkey. Let stand until cold. Combine thickened milk mixture and turkey mixture.

Preheat oven to 425F (220C). Line a baking sheet with parchment paper. Melt remaining butter. Lay 3 sheets of phyllo pastry flat on a tea towel, brushing in between each sheet with melted butter. Spread with 1/3 of filling to within 1/2 inch of edges; repeat twice more using pastry and filling. Fold in all edges and roll up in a roll with aid of tea towel and roll onto a prepared baking sheet. Brush with remaining butter. Bake in oven 20 to 25 minutes or until golden brown. Cut in slices and serve. Makes 6 servings.

Fruit Pork Pillows

2 tablespoons butter
2 (1-lb.) pork tenderloins, cut in 4 pieces each
3 tablespoons whipping cream, whipped
1 cup chopped dried apricots
1 lb. puff pastry, thawed
2/3 cup sweet cherries, pitted, halved
Fresh sage leaves
Salt and ground black pepper to taste
1 egg, beaten

Preheat oven to 400F (205C). Line a baking sheet with waxed paper. Melt butter in a large skillet. Fry pork pieces quickly 1 minute, turning once, to seal. Drain on paper towels and cool.

In a bowl, whip cream until thick. Fold in apricots. Cut pastry in 8 pieces. Roll out 1 piece very thinly and trim to a square. Spread 1/8 of apricot filling over center. Top with 4 cherry halves, 1 sage leaf and a piece of pork. Season with salt and pepper.

Brush pastry edges with beaten egg; fold pastry over pork and seal well. Invert onto prepared baking sheet and brush with egg. Repeat to make another 7 pillows. Roll out and cut trimmings in holly leaves and berries and decorate each pillow. Brush with egg. Bake in oven 20 to 30 minutes or until pastry has risen and is golden brown. Garnish with remaining cherries and sage leaves and serve hot. Makes 8 servings.

Turkey Risotto

1/4 cup butter
1 large onion, sliced
1 clove garlic, crushed
4 oz. button mushrooms, sliced
1 cup Italian risotto rice
1 teaspoon saffron strands
1 teaspoon salt
1/2 teaspoon ground black pepper
1-3/4 cups turkey stock
2/3 cup white wine
1 small red bell pepper
1 small yellow bell pepper
10 oz. cooked turkey
2 tablespoons shredded Gruyere cheese
1 tablespoon chopped fresh parsley
Small red and yellow bell pepper rings and
   parsley to garnish

Melt butter in a saucepan. Add onion, garlic and mushrooms and cook 2 minutes or until tender. Stir in rice and cook another 2 minutes. Add saffron, salt, pepper, stock and wine. Bring to a boil, stirring constantly, then cover and cook very gently 15 minutes. Broil peppers until skin is charred and peppers are tender. Remove stalk, seeds and skin and cut peppers in fine strips. Cut turkey in bite-sized pieces.

Add turkey and peppers to risotto. Stir carefully to distribute ingredients. Cover and cook another 5 minutes or until rice is tender and mixture is creamy but not dry. Arrange on a warmed serving plate. Sprinkle with cheese and parsley. Garnish with bell pepper rings and parsley and serve hot. Makes 4 to 6 servings.

Turkey Soup

1 turkey, chicken or goose carcass
1/3 cup butter
3 slices bacon, chopped
1 onion, chopped
2 carrots, chopped
3 stalks celery, chopped
2 leeks, sliced
Cold water
1/4 to 1/2 cup all-purpose flour
1 teaspoon salt
1 teaspoon ground black pepper
2/3 cup sherry or wine
Croutons and chopped parsley to garnish

Preheat oven to 425F (220C). Break up carcass in pieces, reserving any pieces of meat. Place carcass in a roasting pan with skin or any leftover bones. Bake 45 to 50 minutes or until bones are golden brown.

Melt 2 tablespoons of butter in a large saucepan. Add bacon, onion, carrots, celery and leeks. Fry quickly until vegetables are lightly browned, stirring frequently. Add carcass and cover with enough cold water to cover all ingredients. Bring to a boil. Cover and simmer 2 to 3 hours.

Strain stock into a large bowl. Cool overnight. Remove fat from top. Melt remaining butter in a saucepan. Stir in flour and cook 1 minute, stirring constantly. Gradually add stock. Bring to a boil, stirring constantly, and cook 5 minutes. Add reserved turkey meat, salt, pepper and sherry or wine. Garnish with croutons and chopped parsley and serve hot. Makes 6 servings.

Red Currant & Clementine Duck

1 (5-lb.) oven-ready duck
Salt
2 tablespoons butter
3 shallots, finely chopped
1-1/4 cups rosé wine
1/2 teaspoon salt
1/2 teaspoon ground black pepper
1 teaspoon whole-grain mustard
1 tablespoon chopped fresh oregano
Finely grated peel and juice 2 clementines
2 tablespoons red currant jelly
3/4 cup red currants, thawed
1 egg, beaten
1-1/2 cups fresh white bread crumbs

Preheat oven to 425F (220C). Remove giblets from duck. Chop liver and reserve. Prepare stock with remainder. Pierce skin all over with a fork; rub salt into skin. Place duck in a roasting pan. Bake in oven 1 hour or until golden brown. Remove and cool 15 minutes. Strain fat from roasting pan. Meanwhile, melt butter in a saucepan. Fry reserved liver and shallots quickly, stirring constantly, until shallots are tender. Stir in wine, salt, pepper and mustard. Bring to a boil and cook 5 minutes. Pour mixture into a roasting pan. Mix with juices and strain back into saucepan. Stir in oregano, clementine peel and juice and red currant jelly.

Using a sharp knife, cut off legs and wings from duck. Slice breast in thin slices and arrange in a warm ovenproof dish. Pour over sauce and red currants. Cover dish with lid or foil. Brush legs and wings with egg; coat each in bread crumbs and arrange in roasting pan. Return to oven 20 to 30 minutes or until crisp and golden brown. Arrange in dish with breast meat and sauce. Makes 4 servings.

Vegetable-Turkey Kebabs

8 oz. cooked turkey breast
3 small zucchini
1 ear of corn, thawed if frozen
8 cherry tomatoes
8 slices bacon
Hot cooked pasta, if desired
Rosemary sprigs to garnish

Marinade:
2 tablespoons almond oil
1/2 teaspoon salt
1/2 teaspoon ground black pepper
1 teaspoon Dijon-style mustard
2 teaspoons honey
1 tablespoon chopped fresh rosemary
1 tablespoon raspberry vinegar

To prepare marinade, in a bowl, place almond oil, salt, pepper, mustard, honey, rosemary and vinegar. Beat well to blend.

Cut turkey in even bite-sized pieces. Slice zucchini and corn in thick slices. Add turkey, zucchini, corn and tomatoes to marinade; stir well to coat evenly. Cover with plastic wrap and refrigerate at least 1 hour. Stretch bacon slices flat with a knife and cut each slice in 3 pieces. Remove turkey pieces from marinade and wrap each in a piece of bacon.

Using 4 long wooden skewers, thread a mixture of ingredients onto each. Brush well with marinade and arrange on a grill pan lined with foil. Broil under a hot grill for 5 to 6 minutes, turning frequently, or until bacon is crisp and vegetables are just tender. Serve immediately on hot cooked pasta, if desired. Garnish with rosemary. Makes 4 servings.

—— Broccoli & Cauliflower Crumble ——

8 oz. cauliflower florets
8 oz. broccoli florets
Hard-cooked egg wedges and parsley sprigs to
   garnish

Topping:
2 tablespoons butter
1 cup soft white bread crumbs
1 tablespoon chopped fresh parsley
1 hard-cooked egg, sieved

Sauce:
2 tablespoons butter
1/4 cup all-purpose flour
1-1/4 cups milk
1/2 teaspoon salt
1/2 teaspoon ground black pepper

To prepare topping, heat butter in a skillet. Add bread crumbs and fry until golden brown and crisp. In a bowl, combine bread crumbs, parsley and sieved egg.

To prepare sauce, place butter, flour, milk, salt and pepper in a saucepan. Whisk over moderate heat until thick. Cook 1 to 2 minutes. Keep warm.

In a saucepan, cook cauliflower and broccoli in boiling salted water 3 to 4 minutes or until just tender. Drain and place in a warmed serving dish. Pour over sauce and sprinkle with topping. Garnish with egg wedges and parsley sprigs. Makes 4 to 6 servings.

Brussel Sprouts with Almonds

1 lb. small Brussel sprouts
2 tablespoons butter
1/4 cup flaked almonds
1 clove garlic, crushed
1 teaspoon grated lemon peel
1 teaspoon fresh lemon juice
1/2 teaspoon salt
1/2 teaspoon ground black pepper
Lemon twists and herb sprigs to garnish

Trim tops off sprouts and cut across top of each. In a saucepan, cook sprouts in boiling salted water 4 to 5 minutes or until just tender. Drain well and place in a warmed serving dish.

Meanwhile, melt butter in a skillet. Add flaked almonds and garlic. Fry until almonds are golden brown. Stir in lemon peel, juice, salt and pepper and mix well.

Sprinkle almonds over sprouts; stir gently to mix. Garnish with lemon twists and herb sprigs. Makes 4 servings.

Soufflé Potatoes

4 large potatoes
2 tablespoons butter
2 tablespoons half and half
1 teaspoon salt
1/2 teaspoon ground black pepper
1/2 teaspoon grated nutmeg
2 eggs, separated
Parsley sprigs to garnish

Preheat oven to 425F (220C). Scrub potatoes until skins are clean and remove any 'eyes.' Using a small sharp knife, pierce each potato several times and arrange on a baking sheet. Bake in oven 1 hour or until potatoes are tender.

Cut each potato in half. Carefully scoop out potato flesh and place in a bowl. Replace potato skins on baking sheet and bake 10 to 15 minutes or until crisp and golden. Meanwhile, mash or beat potato flesh until smooth. Add butter, half and half, salt, pepper, nutmeg and egg yolks. Mash or beat until thoroughly blended.

In a small bowl, stiffly whisk egg whites until stiff. Using a spatula, gently fold egg whites into potato mixture until evenly mixed. Fill each potato skin with mixture and bake 10 to 15 minutes or until risen and lightly browned. Garnish with parsley sprigs and serve immediately. Makes 8 servings.

Variation:
Add 1/2 cup chopped crispy bacon, shredded cheese or chopped mixed fresh herbs to potato mixture.

Creamed Spinach & Celery

2 lb. fresh spinach
6 stalks celery
2 tablespoons butter
1 teaspoon grated nutmeg
1/3 cup whipping cream
1/4 teaspoon salt
1/2 teaspoon ground black pepper
Additional celery slices and leaves to garnish

Stem and wash spinach. Wash and thinly slice celery. In 2 saucepans, cook celery and spinach separately in boiling salted water until just tender. Drain thoroughly. Press excess water from spinach.

Line bottom and sides of 8 warm individual soufflé dishes with whole spinach leaves. Coarsely chop remaining spinach. Melt butter in a saucepan. Add nutmeg, whipping cream, salt and pepper and bring to a boil. Add chopped spinach and toss well.

Half-fill each soufflé dish with spinach mixture and cover each with a layer of celery. Fill each to top with remaining chopped spinach. Press firmly. Invert spinach molds to serve. Garnish with celery slices and leaves. Makes 8 servings.

Baked Potato Layer

2 lb. medium-size potatoes
2 tablespoons butter
1 clove garlic, crushed
1 teaspoon salt
1 teaspoon ground black pepper
1 cup shredded Cheddar cheese (4 oz.)
1-1/4 cups milk
2/3 cup half and half
1 large egg, beaten
Parsley sprigs to garnish

Preheat oven to 375F (190C). Using a sharp knife, peel and very thinly slice potatoes or use a food processor fitted with a fine slicing blade. Lightly butter a 9-inch shallow oven-proof dish using 1/2 of butter.

Arrange a layer of potato slices over bottom and up sides of dish. Sprinkle with some of garlic, salt, pepper and cheese. Continue to layer until all these ingredients have been used, finishing with a layer of potatoes and a sprinkling of cheese.

In a bowl, whisk milk, half and half and egg until smooth. Pour over potato layer and dot with remaining butter. Bake 1 hour or until golden brown and potatoes are tender. Garnish with parsley sprigs and serve hot. Makes 4 servings.

Glazed Carrots & Onions

12 small even-sized carrots
16 pickling onions
1 teaspoon salt
1/4 cup turkey or chicken stock
1 tablespoon superfine sugar
2 tablespoons butter
1 tablespoon chopped fresh parsley
Herb sprigs to garnish

Peel and trim carrots so they are all even in size. Peel and trim onions. In 2 saucepans, cook carrots and onions separately in boiling salted water 5 to 8 minutes or until just tender. Drain well.

In a medium saucepan, combine stock, sugar and butter. Heat gently, stirring until sugar has dissolved and butter has melted. Boil rapidly until mixture is reduced by half.

Add carrots, onions and parsley. Toss well in glaze and arrange on a warmed serving dish. Garnish with herb sprigs. Makes 4 servings.

Round Christmas Pudding

3 cups mixed dried fruit
1/2 cup chopped prunes
1/3 cup chopped glacé cherries
1/2 cup chopped almonds
1/4 cup grated carrot
1/4 cup grated cooking apple
Finely grated peel and juice 1 orange
1 tablespoon molasses
1 tablespoon brandy
1/3 cup stout
1 egg, beaten
1/4 cup butter, melted
1/3 cup dark-brown sugar
3/4 teaspoon ground allspice
1/2 cup all-purpose flour
1 cup soft white bread crumbs
Holly sprigs to decorate
Additional brandy
1 recipe Brandy Butter, opposite page

Combine mixed fruit, prunes, cherries, almonds, carrot, apple, orange peel and juice, molasses, brandy and stout. Stir in egg, butter, brown sugar, allspice, flour and bread crumbs. Cover with plastic wrap and refrigerate.

Using a 5-inch buttered spherical mold or a rice steamer mold lined with a double thickness of foil, fill each half of mold with mixture. Place 2 halves together, securing mold tightly.

Half-fill a saucepan with water. Bring to a boil and place mold in so water comes just below seam of mold. Cover and simmer 6 hours. Cool in mold, then turn out. When cold, wrap in foil. To reheat, unwrap and replace in mold. Cook as before in simmering water 2 to 3 hours. Decorate with holly. Warm brandy, spoon over pudding and light. Serve with Brandy Butter. Makes 8 servings.

Brandy Butter

1 cup unsalted butter
1 cup superfine sugar
1/3 cup brandy
Holly sprig to decorate

In a bowl or food processor fitted with a metal blade, beat or process butter until white and creamy. Add sugar and beat or process until light and fluffy.

Add brandy a drop at a time, beating continuously, until enough has been added to well-flavor butter. Take care mixture does not curdle through overbeating.

Spoon butter into a glass dish and serve with a spoon or spread about 1/2 inch thick over a flat dish and chill until hard. Using a fancy cutter, cut in shapes and arrange on a chilled serving dish. Decorate with holly. Makes 8 servings.

Christmas Cake

Cake:
6-3/4 cups mixed dried fruit
3/4 cup quartered glacé cherries
1/2 cup cut mixed peel
3/4 cup flaked almonds
Finely grated peel and juice 1 orange
1/2 cup brandy or sherry
3 cups all-purpose flour
1 tablespoon ground mixed spice
2/3 cup ground almonds
1-1/2 cups dark-brown sugar
1-1/2 cups butter, softened
2 tablespoons molasses
5 eggs

Decoration:
3 tablespoons apricot jam, boiled, sieved
1-3/4 lb. marzipan
2-lb. ready-to-roll fondant icing (sugar paste)
Red and green food colorings
Red and green ribbon

Preheat oven to 275F (135C). Line a 2-1/2-inch deep 8-inch-square or 2-1/2-inch deep 9-inch-round cake pan with a double thickness of greased parchment paper, extending parchment paper above sides of pan. Place pan on a double parchment paper-lined baking sheet. In a large bowl, combine dried fruit, cherries, mixed peel and flaked almonds until well mixed. Add orange peel and juice and brandy or sherry; mix well.

In another bowl, combine flour, mixed spice, ground almonds, brown sugar, butter, molasses and eggs with a wooden spoon, then beat until smooth and glossy. Add mixed fruit to cake mixture; stir until evenly mixed.

Spoon mixture into prepared pan. Level top with back of a metal spoon, making a slight depression in center. Bake in oven 3-1/4 to 3-1/2 hours. Test with a skewer; when inserted in center, skewer should come out clean. Cool in pan. Invert cake, remove paper and place on a cake plate.

Brush top and side of cake with apricot jam. Knead marzipan and roll out to 1/4-inch thickness. Cover top and sides of cake; trim to fit at bottom. Roll out fondant icing on a lightly sugared surface. Cover cake. Press icing over top and down side of cake. Trim off excess icing at bottom.

Knead trimmings together; color 1/3 red and remainder green with food colorings. Make tiny berries with some of the red icing. Roll and cut out holly leaves from green icing. Mark in veins with knife; let stand until set. Arrange on top of cake with berries. Cut out 'NOEL' from red icing and place on cake. Let cake stand until dry. Tie with ribbon. Makes 40 servings.

Festive Mince Pies

1-1/2 cups mincemeat
1 egg white
Red and green food colorings

Pastry:
3 cups all-purpose flour
3/4 cup butter
2 tablespoons superfine sugar
1 egg yolk
Cold water

Preheat oven to 400F (205C). To prepare pastry, sift flour into a bowl. Cut butter into flour finely until mixture resembles bread crumbs. Using a fork, stir in sugar, egg yolk and enough cold water to form a soft dough. Knead on a lightly floured surface.

Roll out pastry thinly and cut out 20 (3-inch) rounds and 20 (2-inch) rounds. Line 20 tart pans with large pastry circles. Prick bottom of each with a fork and half-fill with mincemeat. Brush edges of each pastry lid with water, invert and press on top of tart to seal edges. Pierce a hole in center to allow steam to escape. Using all pastry trimmings, roll out thinly. Using a holly leaf cutter, cut out 40 holly leaves; mark veins with a knife. Roll tiny balls of pastry to form berries. Brush top of each mince pie with egg white. Arrange holly leaves and berries on top.

Bake in oven 15 minutes until cooked but not pale. Divide egg white between 2 cups; color 1 red and 1 green with food colorings. Brush leaves green and berries red. Bake in oven another 5 minutes. Cool on a wire rack. Makes 20 pies.

Southern Comfort Cake

1-1/4 cups butter
1/2 cup plus 2 tablespoons light corn syrup
1-1/4 cups Southern Comfort, sherry or cider
Finely grated peel and juice 1 orange
Finely grated peel and juice 1 lemon
6-1/4 cups mixed dried fruit
2-1/2 cups chopped dried apricots
2-1/4 cups chopped dried dates
3/4 teaspoon baking soda
3 eggs
3-1/2 cups whole-wheat self-rising flour
2 teaspoons ground allspice
1/2 cup apricot jam, boiled, sieved
2-1/4 cups assorted nuts such as pecans, brazil
    nuts, hazelnuts, pine nuts
Whole dried apricot and dates
Holly sprigs to decorate
Ribbon

Grease and double-line a 10" x 8" x 2" baking pan with waxed paper. Place pan on a double-waxed-paper-lined baking sheet. In a large saucepan, combine butter, corn syrup, Southern Comfort, sherry or cider and orange and lemon peel and juice. Heat until almost boiling. Stir in mixed fruit, apricots and dates, stirring until well blended. Let stand until almost cold. Preheat oven to 300F (150C). Add soda, eggs, flour and allspice and stir until mixture is thoroughly mixed.

Spoon mixture into prepared pan. Level top and bake in oven 2-1/4 to 2-1/2 hours or until cake feels firm in center. Test with a skewer; when inserted in center, skewer should come out clean. Cool in pan, invert and wrap in foil until needed. Cut cake in 6 pieces. Brush each piece with apricot jam. Arrange nuts and fruit over top and glaze with remaining jam. Let stand until set. Decorate with holly sprigs tied with ribbon. Makes 6 individual cakes.

Mini Christmas Cakes

1 (8-inch) square Christmas Cake, page 64, or
    Glacé Fruit Cake, page 96
4 (4-inch) square cake cards
1/3 cup apricot jam, boiled, sieved
2 lb. white marzipan
Red, green and silver food colorings
Cornstarch
1 egg white
2-1/4 yards each red, green and silver ribbon
1-1/2 lb. ready-to-roll fondant icing (sugar
    paste)
Powdered sugar
Red, green and silver dragees
Red and green cake candle

Cut cake in 4 small square cakes; place each
on a cake board. Brush evenly with apricot
jam. Cut marzipan in 4 pieces. Color 1 piece
pale pink and 1 pale green with food colorings. Roll out 1 piece at a time to about 6
inches square on a lightly sugared surface.
Place over cake and trim to fit; reserve marzipan trimmings. Let white marzipan cakes dry
in a warm place. Using a crimper dipped in
cornstarch, crimp top and bottom edge of
pink and green cakes.

Color remaining green and pink marzipan
bright green and red by adding a few more
drops of food colorings. Roll out green thinly
and cut out about 20 holly leaves using a holly
leaf cutter. Shape red marzipan in tiny holly
berries. Arrange holly leaves and berries over
top of cake, securing each with some egg
white. Using green and red ribbon, measure
and cut ribbon to fit round outside of each
cake.

Sprinkle surface of fondant icing with powdered sugar. Cut icing in half; place half in a
plastic bag and seal. Knead remaining icing
until smooth; roll out to an 8-inch square.
Place icing over 1 cake with marzipan. With
hands covered with cornstarch, smooth top
and sides and trim off excess icing around
bottom of cake. Repeat to cover second cake.
Knead icing trimmings together.

Press silver and red dragees around top edge
and bottom of cake; secure with egg white, if
necessary. Repeat with green and silver
dragees on remaining cake. Tie silver and
green and silver and red ribbon around each
respective cake; tie with pretty bows.

Roll out icing trimmings on a surface dusted
lightly with cornstarch. Using a tiny star-
shaped cutter, cut out 26 stars. Using food
coloring, paint surfaces of 14 stars silver, 6
stars red and 6 stars green. Let stand until
dry. Arrange green and silver stars on green
and silver cake and red and silver stars on red
and silver cake. Place a candle in center of
each. Let stand until dry. Makes 4 individual
cakes.

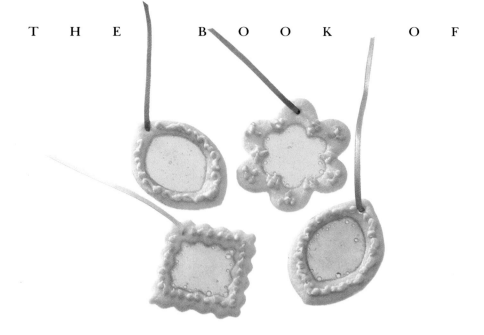

Mobiles

1-1/4 cups all-purpose flour
3 tablespoons custard powder
1/3 cup butter
2 tablespoons plus 2 teaspoons superfine sugar
1 egg white
2 tablespoons lemon juice
8 oz. clear fruit candies
4 (1-oz.) squares white chocolate, melted
Red and green oil-based or powdered food
   colorings
Colored fine ribbons

Preheat oven to 350F (175C). Line 2 baking sheets with parchment paper. Sift flour and custard powder into a bowl. Cut butter into flour mixture finely until mixture resembles bread crumbs. Stir in sugar, egg white and enough lemon juice to make a soft dough. Knead on a lightly floured surface and roll out 1/4 inch thick.

Using a 2-inch fancy cutter, cut out about 20 shapes. Arrange on prepared baking sheets, spacing apart. Using a sharp knife or small matching cutters, cut out each center shape leaving 1/2-inch frame. Make a hole at top of each frame with a drinking straw. Place 1/2 of a fruit candy into center of each. Bake until sweets have melted and filled centers. Cool on baking sheets. Bake center cut-out shapes separately.

Divide chocolate among 3 bowls. Color 1 green, 1 red and green and 1 red with food colorings. When chocolate is thick enough to leave a trail on surface, fill 3 small paper pastry bags with each. Fold down tops and snip off points. Decorate each cookie with swirls, dots or lines of colored chocolate. When set, peel off parchment paper. Thread different lengths of ribbon through holes and hang up near the light so that colored centers shine. Makes 20 mobiles.

Smoked Trout Pâté

4 oz. thinly sliced smoked lake trout
12 oz. smoked trout fillets
1 cup fresh white bread crumbs
1/2 (8-oz.) pkg. Neufchâtel cheese, softened
1/4 cup unsalted butter, melted
1/2 teaspoon ground black pepper
1 teaspoon finely grated lemon peel
3 tablespoons sherry or brandy
1 tablespoon chopped fresh dill
1 tablespoon chopped fresh tarragon
Lemon twists and dill sprigs to garnish

Line bottom and sides of a 1-lb. loaf pan with plastic wrap.

Trim sliced smoked lake trout to fit bottom and sides of pan. Using a food processor fitted with a metal blade, process trout fillets, bread crumbs, Neufchâtel cheese, butter, pepper, lemon peel, sherry or brandy, dill and tarragon until smooth. Or beat all ingredients in a bowl.

Spoon pâté mixture into prepared pan. Press down firmly and level. Cover top with plastic wrap and refrigerate until firm. Remove plastic wrap. Invert pâté onto a serving plate. Remove remaining plastic wrap and cut in thin slices. Garnish with lemon twists and dill sprigs. Makes 8 servings.

Flavored Cheeses

Port & Peppercorn Cheese:
1/2 (8-oz.) pkg. Neufchâtel cheese, softened
3/4 cup shredded Cheddar cheese (3 oz.)
2 tablespoons ruby port
Chives and 2 teaspoons pink peppercorns

Combine cheeses and port until evenly blended. Shape in a round ball, then press in a disc shape. Garnish with chives and pink peppercorns.

Blue Cheese:
1/2 (8-oz.) pkg. cream cheese, softened
3/4 cup shredded blue Stilton cheese (3 oz.)
1 teaspoon Dijon-style mustard
1/4 teaspoon cayenne pepper
1/4 cup sunflower seeds
1/4 cup chopped walnuts

Combine cheeses, mustard and cayenne pepper until evenly mixed. Divide mixture in half; mold each half in a cylinder shape. Roll 1 in sunflower seeds and other in walnuts.

Herbed Cheese:
1/2 (8-oz.) pkg. cream cheese
1 small clove garlic, crushed
2 teaspoons snipped chives
1 teaspoon chopped fresh oregano
1 teaspoon chopped fresh thyme
1/4 teaspoon ground black pepper
Bay leaves and 1 teaspoon green peppercorns

Combine 1/3 of cream cheese, garlic, herbs and black pepper until well blended. Shape remaining cheese in a ball and flatten in a thin round. Shape herb mixture in a ball and place in center of cheese round. Press plain cheese over herbed mixture and form in a ball. Garnish with bay leaves and peppercorns.

Refrigerate all cheeses until firm. Use within 10 days. Makes 4 cheeses.

Pickled Mixed Vegetables

1 cucumber, peeled
8 zucchini, trimmed
1 lb. pickling onions, peeled
1 lb. red and green bell peppers, seeded
1 lb. green or red tomatoes, peeled, seeded
3 tablespoons salt
Red bell pepper rings and tarragon sprigs to
    garnish

Spiced Vinegar:
2 cups light-brown sugar
1 teaspoon celery seeds
1 teaspoon turmeric
1 teaspoon ground mace
1 tablespoon plus 1 teaspoon mustard seeds
2-1/2 cups tarragon, cider or wine vinegar

Cut all vegetables in thin slices. Arrange in a large bowl, sprinkling salt in between layers. Cover with plastic wrap and refrigerate 3 hours. Drain vegetables and rinse thoroughly under running water, then drain thoroughly.

To prepare Spiced Vinegar, combine all ingredients in a stainless steel or enamel saucepan. Stir over gentle heat until sugar has dissolved. Bring to a boil and boil 3 minutes. Add vegetables to Spiced Vinegar. Bring to a boil, stirring occasionally. Cook 1 minute. Spoon into a serving bowl. Serve hot or cold. Garnish with bell pepper rings and tarragon sprigs. Makes 10 to 12 servings.

Ginger Marron Glacé

Pavlova:
3 egg whites
1 cup superfine sugar
1 teaspoon white vinegar
1 teaspoon orange flower water
1 teaspoon cornstach
Mint sprigs to decorate

Filling:
1-1/4 cups whipping cream
3 pieces preserved stem ginger in syrup,
    chopped
10 whole marrons glacés, cut in pieces
Vanilla ice cream

Preheat oven to 275F (135C). Line 2 baking sheets with parchment paper. Mark 10 (3-inch) circles and invert paper.

In a bowl, whisk egg whites until stiff. Gradually add sugar, whisking well after each addition until thick. In a bowl, blend vinegar, orange flower water and cornstarch. Add to meringue and whisk until very thick and glossy. Place meringue in a large pastry bag fitted with a small star nozzle. Pipe a shell edging around marked lines, then fill in center with a thin layer of meringue. Pipe a second shell edging on top of first edge. Bake 45 minutes. Turn off oven and leave meringues in to cool. Remove when cold. Store in an airtight container until needed.

In a bowl, whip cream until thick. Place 1/2 of whipped cream into pastry bag fitted with a nozzle. Fold chopped ginger into remaining whipped cream and spoon into center of each meringue. Just before serving, top each with balls of ice cream and a marron glacé. Decorate with mint sprigs. Makes 10 servings.

Soufflé Lime & Chocolate Layer

4 eggs, separated
1/3 cup superfine sugar
1 tablespoon plain gelatin
3 tablespoons water
Finely grated peel and juice 1 lime
2 (1-oz.) squares semi-sweet chocolate, melted
1-1/4 cups whipping cream
Chocolate curls and lime peel to decorate

In a bowl, combine egg yolks and sugar. Set over a saucepan of simmering water. Whisk until pale and thick. Remove bowl from pan. Continue to whisk until mixture leaves a trail when whisk is lifted. In a small bowl, sprinkle gelatin over water and let soften 2 to 3 minutes. Stand bowl in saucepan of hot water and stir until dissolved and quite hot.

Stir gelatin into egg yolk mixture until well blended. Pour 1/2 of mixture into another bowl. Stir grated lime peel and juice into 1 mixture and chocolate into remaining mixture until well blended. In a small bowl, whisk egg whites until stiff. In another small bowl, whip cream until thick. Add 1/2 of egg whites and cream to each mixture and fold in carefully until evenly blended.

Place alternate spoonfuls of each mixture into 8 small glasses. Let stand until set, then decorate with chocolate curls and lime twists. Makes 8 servings.

Rose Custard Creams

1-1/4 cups milk
1-1/4 cups whipping cream
2 eggs
2 egg yolks
2 tablespoons plus 2 teaspoons superfine sugar
2 tablespoons plus 2 teaspoons rosé water

Marinated Fruit:
1 tablespoon plus 1 teaspoon rose water
1 tablespoon plus 1 teaspoon rosé wine
2 tablespoons plus 2 teaspoons powdered sugar
Petals from 2 scented roses
1 cup strawberries, sliced
1 cup raspberries, thawed if frozen
1 starfruit, sliced

Preheat oven to 300F (150C). In a saucepan, bring milk and whipping cream almost to boiling point.

In a bowl, beat eggs and egg yolks. Pour milk mixture into eggs, stirring well. Add sugar and rose water and stir until well blended. Divide mixture among 8 individual soufflé dishes. Stand dishes in a roasting pan and half-fill pan with cold water. Bake in oven about 1 hour or until custard has set. Remove dishes from water and refrigerate until cold.

To prepare marinated fruit, mix rose water, wine, powdered sugar and rose petals in a bowl. Add fruit; stir until well mixed. Cover with plastic wrap and chill until ready to serve. Turn custards out onto individual plates and serve with marinated fruit. Makes 8 servings.

Tipsy Fruit Jelly

3 lemons
1-1/4 cups water
1/2 cup superfine sugar
2/3 cup claret
2 tablespoons plain gelatin
1/4 cup hot water
12 oz. mixed fresh fruit such as grapes,
  lychees, pineapple, clementines, cut up
Additional fresh fruit and whipped cream to
  decorate

Using a vegetable peeler or sharp knife, pare peel from lemons. Squeeze juice. In a saucepan, combine peel and water and bring to a boil. Add sugar; stir until dissolved. Let stand until cold, then strain. Stir in lemon juice. Pour 1/3 of lemon mixture into a bowl. Add claret, stir until blended.

In a small bowl, sprinkle gelatin over hot water. Let stand until softened. Place bowl in a saucepan of hot water. Stir until dissolved and quite hot. Add 1/2 of gelatin to claret mixture, stirring well, and the remainder to lemon mixture, stirring well. Halve grapes and lychees, remove seeds and pits. Peel and slice pineapple and clementines.

Arrange 1/4 of mixed fruit in bottom of 6 individual molds. Spoon enough lemon jelly over fruit to cover. Refrigerate until set. Arrange a second layer of fruit over set jelly layer and cover with claret jelly; refrigerate until set. Repeat to make another lemon fruit layer and claret fruit layer. Refrigerate until firmly set. Remove from molds by dipping into hand-hot water and invert onto a plate. Decorate with fresh fruit and piped whipped cream. Makes 6 servings.

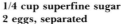

Amaretti Cheese Whip

1/4 cup superfine sugar
2 eggs, separated
1-1/4 cups mascarpone cream cheese, beaten
Finely grated peel 1 tangerine
3/4 cup chopped mixed glacé fruits
1/4 cup broken Amaretti cookies (macaroons)
1 tablespoon plus 1 teaspoon Amaretto liqueur
2/3 cup whipping cream

Decoration:
**Glacé fruits and Amaretti cookies (macaroons)
to decorate**

In a bowl, combine sugar and egg yolks. Set over a saucepan of simmering water. Whisk until mixture leaves a trail when whisk is lifted.

Stir in cream cheese, tangerine peel, chopped glacé fruits, broken Amaretti cookies and liqueur. In a small bowl, whisk egg whites until stiff. In another small bowl, whip whipping cream until thick. Add egg whites and whipped cream to cream cheese mixture and fold in carefully until mixture is evenly blended. Cover with plastic wrap and chill until needed.

Just before serving, divide mixture among 6 to 8 small dishes. Decorate with glacé fruit and Amaretti cookies. Makes 6 to 8 servings.

Lychee & Port Ice Cream

1/2 cup superfine sugar
2/3 cup ruby port
20 fresh lychees or 1 (15-oz.) can lychees
1 tablespoon plus 1 teaspoon lime juice
1-1/4 cups whipping cream
Fresh or canned lychees and lime peel twists to
    decorate

In a saucepan, combine sugar and port. Heat gently, stirring occasionally, until sugar has dissolved. Peel lychees and remove pits or drain canned lychees. Add lychees to port mixture. Bring to a boil, cover and cook very gently 2 minutes. Let stand until completely cold.

Using a food processor fitted with a metal blade, process port and lychees until smooth. Pour mixture into a sieve set over a bowl and rub mixture through using a wooden spoon. Stir in lime juice. In a bowl, whip cream until thick. Add port mixture to whipped cream and fold in until evenly blended. Pour mixture into a plastic container, cover and freeze 1 to 2 hours or until mixture is almost frozen but still soft.

Return mixture to food processor. Process until smooth and creamy. Return mixture to plastic container and freeze until firm. Scoop ice cream to serve. Decorate with lychees and lime peel. Makes 6 servings.

Frostie Fruit Brûlées

2 oranges
2 eating apples
2 figs
2 bananas
1 cup seedless grapes, halved
2 tablespoons Marsala wine
2-1/2 cups whipping cream
3/4 cup superfine sugar
1/4 cup boiling water

Using a sharp knife, cut orange peel away from flesh including white pith. Cut in between membrane to remove segments; place in a bowl. Cut apples into quarters; remove cores and slice thinly. Cut figs in thin wedges and slice bananas.

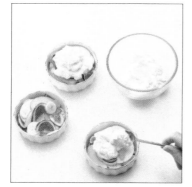

Gently combine all fruit and wine in bowl. Divide fruit among 6 individual dishes. In a bowl, whip cream until very thick. Spoon whipped cream evenly over fruit. Chill until ready to serve.

In a saucepan, heat sugar and water, stirring occasionally, until sugar has dissolved. Boil rapidly until syrup turns a golden brown color. Allow bubbles to subside, then drizzle caramel over top of fruit brûlées. Serve immediately. Makes 6 servings.

Festive Cheesecake

1-1/2 (8-oz.) pkgs. cream cheese
2/3 cup fromage frais
2 eggs, separated
1 tablespoon plus 1 teaspoon Grenadine syrup
1/3 cup Marsala wine
1 tablespoon plus 2 teaspoons plain gelatin
3 tablespoons water
1 starfruit, sliced
2 figs, sliced
10 kumquats, sliced
Melon balls
Seedless green and black grapes, halved
Holly sprigs and additional kumquat slices to
  decorate

Crust:
1/4 cup butter
1 tablespoon light corn syrup
2 cups vanilla wafer crumbs

To prepare crust, gently heat butter and syrup in a saucepan until melted. Stir in vanilla wafer crumbs and press into bottom of a 9-inch spring-form pan. To prepare filling, beat cream cheese, fromage frais, egg yolks, 1 tablespoon Grenadine syrup and 2 tablespoons wine in a bowl until smooth. In a small bowl, sprinkle gelatin over water and let stand until softened. Stand bowl in saucepan of hot water and stir until dissolved and quite hot. Stir gelatin into cheesecake mixture and let stand until thickened. In a bowl, whisk egg whites until stiff. Fold egg whites into cheesecake mixture until well blended and smooth. Pour over crust. Shake to level top and chill until set.

In a bowl, place all fruits. In a saucepan, heat remaining Grenadine syrup and wine until hot but not boiling. Pour over fruit and let stand until cold. Drain liquid into saucepan. Arrange fruit over top of cheesecake. Boil liquid until syrupy, brush fruit to glaze. Cut in slices to serve. Decorate with holly sprigs and additional kumquat slices. Makes 8 servings.

Chocolate Cherry Slice

Cake:
6 (1-oz.) squares semi-sweet chocolate
4 eggs
1/4 cup superfine sugar
1/3 cup all-purpose flour

Filling:
1 cup unsweetened marron purée
4 (1-oz.) squares semi-sweet chocolate, melted
1-1/4 cups whipping cream
3 tablespoons cherry jam
1 cup sweet cherries, pitted, halved

Preheat oven to 350F (175C). Line a 13" x 9" jelly roll pan with waxed paper. To prepare cake, break up chocolate; place in a bowl over a saucepan of hand-hot water. Stir occasionally until melted and smooth.

In a bowl, whisk eggs and sugar until thick and pale and a trail is left when whisk is lifted. Stir in chocolate until evenly blended. Sift in flour and fold in gently until evenly mixed. Pour mixture into prepared pan and shake to level. Bake in oven 20 to 25 minutes or until firm to touch. Remove from oven. Cover with a damp tea towel and let stand until cold. To prepare filling, process marron in a food processor fitted with a metal blade to a purée. Add chocolate and process until smooth. In a small bowl, whip cream until thick. Place 1/3 of whipped cream into a pastry bag fitted with small star nozzle. Fold remaining whipped cream into chocolate mixture.

Remove cake from pan. Remove paper, trim edges and cut into 3 short strips across width. Spread 2 strips of cake with jam. Cover each with 1/3 of filling. Spread smoothly. Arrange 1/3 of cherry halves on each and stack layers on a serving plate. Top with remaining cake layer. Spread top and sides of cake evenly with remaining filling and pipe scrolls of whipping cream around top edge. Decorate with remaining cherry halves. Chill until needed. Makes 10 servings.

English Trifle

2 eggs
2 egg yolks
1 tablespoon plus 2 teaspoons superfine sugar
1-1/4 cups milk
1 teaspoon vanilla extract
2 tablespoons Madeira wine
1 tablespoon brandy
20 sponge fingers
2 tablespoons raspberry jam
1-1/2 cups raspberries, thawed if frozen
1-1/4 cups whipping cream
Angelica leaves to decorate
Vanilla cookies, if desired

To prepare custard, whisk whole eggs, egg yolks and sugar in a bowl until well blended. In a saucepan, bring milk and vanilla to boil. Pour over eggs in bowl, stirring thoroughly. Rinse out saucepan and strain custard through a sieve back into saucepan. Stirring continuously, cook over a gentle heat until thick but do not boil. Let stand until cold. In a small bowl, mix wine and brandy. Dip 1 sponge finger at a time into wine mixture. Spread with some jam and sandwich together with another dipped sponge finger. Place in bottom of a glass dish.

Repeat with remaining sponge fingers to cover bottom of dish. Pour remaining wine mixture over sponge fingers and cover with 2/3 of raspberries. In a bowl, whip cream until soft peaks form. Fold 2/3 of whipped cream into cold custard until well blended and smooth. Pour custard over raspberries in bowl. Place remaining whipped cream in a pastry bag fitted with a star nozzle. Pipe a border and decorate with angelica leaves and remaining raspberries. Serve with cookies, if desired. Chill until needed. Makes 8 servings.

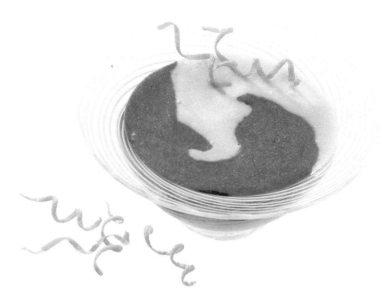

White & Dark Chocolate Pots

4 (1-oz.) squares white chocolate
4 (1-oz.) squares semi-sweet chocolate
4 eggs, separated
1 tablespoon rum
1 tablespoon Cointreau liqueur
Orange peel spirals to decorate

Break up each chocolate and place in a separate bowl. Set each over a saucepan of hand-hot water. Stir occasionally until melted and smooth. Stir 2 egg yolks into each. Stir rum into semi-sweet chocolate and Cointreau into white chocolate until evenly blended.

In a bowl, stiffly beat egg whites. Add 1/2 to each chocolate mixture. Fold in carefully until each mixture is evenly blended and smooth.

Spoon alternate spoonfuls of each mixture evenly into 8 small dessert dishes. Leave in a cool place to set. Decorate with orange peel spirals. Makes 8 servings.

Festive Meringues

1-1/2 cups mixed glacé fruits, chopped
2 tablespoons plus 2 teaspoons Strega liqueur
1 cup whipping cream
1/4 cup plain yogurt
1 starfruit, thinly sliced, to decorate

Meringue:
2 egg whites
1/2 cup superfine sugar

Preheat oven to 250F (120C). Line 2 baking sheets with waxed paper. Draw 5 oval shapes on each using a 2-1/2-inch oval cutter. Invert paper.

In a bowl, whisk egg whites until stiff. Whisk in sugar a little at a time, whisking thoroughly until thick and soft peaks form. Place mixture in a large pastry bag fitted with a medium star nozzle. Pipe shells of meringue around each oval shape, then fill in centers, making sure there are no gaps. Bake in oven 1-1/2 to 2 hours or until meringues are dry, crisp and lift off paper. Cool and store in an airtight container until needed. In a bowl, mix glacé fruit and liqueur and cover.

In a bowl, whip cream and yogurt until thick. Add 2/3 of glacé fruit and all liqueur. Fold in until just mixed. Spoon mixture onto each meringue. Decorate with starfruit slices and remaining glacé fruit. Makes 10 servings.

Saucy Chocolate Pudding

3 (1-oz.) squares white chocolate
3 (1-oz.) squares milk chocolate
3 (1-oz.) squares semi-sweet chocolate
3 egg yolks
2 teaspoons finely grated grapefruit peel
2 teaspoons grapefruit juice
1 tablespoon ginger wine
1 tablespoon Southern Comfort liqueur
3/4 cup softened butter
2/3 cup whipping cream
3 tablespoons fromage frais
Grapefuit slices and mint sprigs to decorate

Grapefruit Sauce:
Finely grated peel and juice 1 grapefruit
Water
2 teaspoons cornstarch
1 tablespoon superfine sugar

Break up each chocolate and place in separate bowls. Set each over a saucepan of hand-hot water. Stir occasionally until melted and smooth. Stir an egg yolk into each. Stir grapefruit peel and juice into white chocolate, ginger wine into milk chocolate and Southern Comfort into semi-sweet chocolate until smooth. Let stand until cold. Beat butter until light and fluffy. Whip cream until thick. Add 1/3 of each to chocolate mixtures and fold in until smooth and evenly blended. Line 6 individual molds with plastic wrap. Divide milk chocolate mixture between molds, making 1 layer.

Repeat with white chocolate layer and finally semi-sweet chocolate layer. Tap molds to level and freeze until firm or until needed. To prepare sauce, measure grapefruit juice and peel and enough water to measure 3/4 cup. Blend juice, cornstarch and sugar. Bring to a boil, stirring constantly. Cook gently 30 seconds; cool. Invert molds 20 minutes before serving. Pour grapefruit sauce around bottom. Decorate with grapefruit and mint. Makes 6 servings.

Kumquat & Cranberry Tarts

3/4 cup superfine sugar
1 cup water
8 oz. kumquats, sliced
1-1/2 cups cranberries
2 (3-oz.) pkgs. cream cheese, softened
1/3 cup plain yogurt
1 teaspoon arrowroot

Walnut Pastry:
1-1/2 cups all-purpose flour
1/2 cup butter
1/2 cup chopped walnuts
1/4 cup superfine sugar
1 egg, beaten

To prepare pastry, sift flour into a bowl. Cut butter into flour finely until mixture resembles fine bread crumbs. Stir in walnuts, sugar and egg. With a fork, mix to form a soft dough.

Knead on a lightly floured surface. Roll out and line 6 (4-1/2-inch) fluted flan pans. Trim edges, prick bottom and chill 30 minutes. Preheat oven to 375F (190C). Gently heat sugar and water in a saucepan until dissolved. Bring to a boil. Add kumquats and cook 3 minutes or until tender. Strain into a sieve. Return 1/3 of syrup to pan; reserve remaining syrup. Add cranberries to syrup in saucepan. Bring to a boil, cover and cook 3 minutes or until tender. Strain into a sieve. Keep syrups and fruits separate. Bake pastries 10 to 15 minutes or until lightly browned. Let stand until cold.

In a bowl, beat cream cheese and yogurt. Spread over bottom of pastries. Arrange alternate circles of kumquats and cranberries on cream cheese mixture. Blend 1/2 teaspoon of arrowroot into each syrup and bring each to boil separately. Glaze kumquats with clear syrup and cranberries with red syrup. Let stand until set. Makes 8 servings.

Tipsy Fruit Fool

1 lb. cooking apples, peeled, sliced
1-1/4 cups dried apricots, pre-soaked
1/4 cup superfine sugar
Peel and juice 3 satsumas
2 tablespoons apricot brandy
1/3 cup fromage frais
Chocolate curls to decorate

In a saucepan, combine apples, apricots, sugar and satsuma peel and juice. Bring to a boil. Cover and cook until apples and apricots are tender. Remove satsuma peel and reserve some for decoration. Let stand until cold.

In a food processor fitted with a metal blade, process apple mixture to a purée. Add apricot brandy and fromage frais and process until well blended. Divide mixture among individual glasses and chill until needed.

Using a sharp knife, cut reserved peel in thin strips. Decorate desserts with satsuma peel strips and chocolate curls. Makes 6 servings.

Mandarin Fig Sorbet

1/2 cup superfine sugar
2/3 cup plus 3 tablespoons water
Peel and juice 4 mandarins
6 green figs
2 teaspoons plain gelatin
2 egg whites
Mandarin shell halves, if desired
Fig slices and mint sprigs to decorate

In a saucepan, heat sugar and 2/3 cup of water, stirring occasionally, until dissolved. Add mandarin peel and figs. Bring to a boil, cover and simmer 10 minutes. Let stand until cold.

Remove mandarin peel. Pour remaining liquid and figs into a food processor fitted with a metal blade. Process to a purée. Sieve mixture into a bowl. In a small bowl, sprinkle gelatin over 3 tablespoons of water and let stand to soften 2 to 3 minutes. Stand bowl in a saucepan of hot water and stir until dissolved and quite hot. Add gelatin and mandarin juice to fig purée; stir until well blended. Pour into a plastic container. Cover and freeze 2 hours or until partially frozen but still soft.

Spoon mixture into food processor and process until creamy, well blended and smooth. In a bowl, whisk egg whites until stiff. Fold in fig purée mixture until smooth. Return mixture to container. Cover and freeze until firm or until needed. Soften 15 minutes before serving in scoops. Serve in mandarin shell halves, if desired. Decorate with fresh fig slices and mint sprigs. Makes 6 servings.

Coffee Chiffon Desserts

1/4 cup butter
3 tablespoons light corn syrup
2 cups vanilla wafer crumbs
2/3 cup whipping cream, whipped, and liqueur
   coffee beans to decorate

Filling:
3 tablespoons cornstarch
1/4 cup superfine sugar
1 tablespoon instant coffee granules
1-1/4 cups milk
2 eggs, separated
1 tablespoon plus 2 teaspoons plain gelatin
3 tablespoons hot water
1-1/4 cups whipping cream

In a saucepan, heat butter and corn syrup until melted. Stir in cookie crumbs and mix together evenly. Divide mixture among 8 plastic wrap-lined tiny molds and press mixture evenly over bottom and up sides of molds. Chill. To prepare filling, mix cornstarch, sugar, coffee and milk in a saucepan. Bring to a boil, stirring constantly, and cook 2 minutes. Remove from heat. Beat in egg yolks. In a small bowl, sprinkle gelatin over hot water; let stand to soften. Set bowl in a saucepan of hot water. Stir until dissolved and quite hot. Stir gelatin into coffee mixture and let stand until thick but not set.

In a small bowl, whisk egg whites until stiff. In a medium bowl, whip cream until thick. Fold egg whites and whipped cream evenly into coffee mixture. Divide mixture among molds, filling each to top. Cover and chill. To serve, invert molds onto serving plates; remove plastic wrap.

To decorate, place whipped cream in a pastry bag fitted with a star nozzle. Pipe around bottom of molds. Decorate with coffee beans. Makes 8 servings.

Amaretti Meringue Bombes

1 tablespoon butter, melted
20 Amaretti cookies (macaroons), crushed
    finely
12 oz. raspberries, thawed if frozen
1 tablespoon plus 1 teaspoon powdered sugar
Additional raspberries and mint sprigs to
    decorate
Amaretti cookies (macaroons), if desired

Filling:
2 cups coarsely crushed meringues
2-1/2 cups whipping cream
1/4 cup Amaretti cookies (macaroons), broken
    in small pieces
1/4 cup maraschino cherries, chopped
1/4 cup chocolate morsels

Brush insides of 8 tiny molds with melted butter. Divide crushed cookies among molds and shake well to coat evenly. Chill.

To prepare filling, mix meringues, cookie pieces, cherries and chocolate in a bowl. Stir to mix well. In another bowl, whip cream to soft peaks. Add meringue mixture to whipped cream and fold in very gently until evenly mixed. Fill each mold with meringue mixture, pressing down to pack evenly. Cover and freeze until needed. In a food processor fitted with a metal blade, process raspberries and powdered sugar to a purée. Sieve raspberry purée into a bowl.

Just before serving, dip each mold into hand-hot water and invert onto serving plates. Decorate with raspberries and mint sprigs. Serve with raspberry purée and cookies, if desired. Makes 8 servings.

Lime & Tangerine Gâteau

3 eggs, separated
2 (4-oz.) pkgs. cream cheese, softened
1/2 cup superfine sugar
Finely grated peel and juice 2 tangerines
Finely grated peel and juice 2 limes
1 tablespoon plus 2 teaspoons plain gelatin
3 tablespoons water
1 pound cake
2/3 cup whipping cream
3 tablespoons fromage frais
1/4 cup chopped pistachio nuts
Lime and tangerine wedges to decorate

To prepare filling, beat egg yolks, cream cheese and sugar in a bowl with a wooden spoon until smooth. Stir in grated fruit peel and 1/2 of juices.

In a small bowl, sprinkle gelatin over water and let stand to soften. Stand bowl in a saucepan of hot water and stir until dissolved and quite hot. Stir into cheese mixture and let stand until thick. Line a deep 7-inch-square pan with plastic wrap. Cut cake into 36 thin slices and line bottom and sides of pan with slices. Sprinkle with 1/3 of fruit juice. In a bowl, whisk egg whites until stiff; fold egg whites into cheese mixture. Pour 1/2 of cheese mixture into pan. Cover with a layer of cake and remaining cheese mixture; sprinkle with 1/3 of fruit juice.

Top with remaining cake and fruit juice. Cover with plastic wrap and chill until set; leave in pan until required. Remove gâteau from pan and remove plastic wrap carefully. In a bowl, whip cream and fromage frais until thick. Spoon 1/4 of mixture into a pastry bag fitted with a small star nozzle. Spread remaining cream evenly over gâteau and press pistachio nuts onto all sides to coat evenly. Pipe a shell border around top of gâteau and decorate with fruit wedges. Makes 12 servings.

Plum & Apple Kuchen

1 (6-oz.) pkg. pizza crust mix
Warm water
2 tablespoons butter, melted
3/4 cup ground almonds
1/4 cup superfine sugar
1 teaspoon ground mixed spice
1 lb. cooking apples, peeled, cored, sliced
2 lb. plums, pitted, halved
1/3 cup plum jam, boiled, sieved
1 tablespoon flaked almonds

Preheat oven to 425F (220C). Butter a flan pan or a baking sheet. Place pizza mix in a bowl. Add warm water as directed by instructions on packet. Knead dough until smooth. Cover and let stand for 5 minutes.

Re-knead dough and roll out to a 12-inch round on a lightly floured surface. Place in buttered flan pan or on baking sheet. Brush dough with butter. In a bowl, mix together almonds, sugar and mixed spice. Sprinkle over dough.

Arrange apple slices and plum halves in a circular pattern over almond mixture. Bake in oven 20 to 30 minutes or until dough is well risen and filling is tender. Cool on a wire rack. Brush with plum jam and sprinkle with flaked almonds. Makes 12 servings.

Rum Truffle Cake

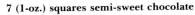

7 (1-oz.) squares semi-sweet chocolate
1/2 cup unsalted butter
1/4 cup dark rum
3 eggs, separated
1/2 cup superfine sugar
3/4 cup all-purpose flour
1/2 cup ground almonds

Filling & Icing:
7 (1-oz.) squares semi-sweet chocolate
1-1/4 cups whipping cream
1 tablespoon dark rum
2 (1-oz.) squares white chocolate, grated

Preheat oven to 350F (175C). Butter and flour a 2-1/2-inch deep 8-inch-round cake pan. Line bottom with a circle of waxed paper.

Place chocolate and butter in a bowl over hand-hot water. Stir occasionally until melted. Add rum and stir well.

Place egg yolks and sugar in a bowl over a saucepan of simmering water. Whisk until thick and pale. Remove bowl from saucepan. Continue to whisk until mixture leaves a trail when whisk has been lifted. Stir chocolate mixture into egg yolk mixture until evenly blended. In a small bowl, mix flour and ground almonds. Add to chocolate mixture; fold in carefully using a spatula.

In a bowl, whisk egg whites until stiff. Fold 1/3 at a time into chocolate mixture until all egg whites are incorporated. Pour mixture into prepared pan. Bake in oven 45 to 55 minutes or until firm to touch in center. Turn out of pan and cool on a wire rack.

To prepare filling, melt 4 squares of chocolate with 1/4 cup of whipping cream in a bowl set over hot water. Stir in rum until well blended. Let stand until cool. To prepare icing, whip 1/2 cup of whipping cream in a bowl until thick. Add 1/2 of rum-chocolate to whipped cream and fold in until smooth.

Cut cake in half. Sandwich together with chocolate icing and spread remainder over top and sides. Chill cake and remaining rum-chocolate mixture in bowl. Melt remaining chocolate with whipping cream in a bowl set over hot water. Stir until smooth and cool until thick. Spread chocolate mixture over cake to cover evenly. Shape rum-chocolate mixture into 16 truffles. Coat in grated white chocolate. Arrange truffles on top of cake and chill to set. Makes 10 servings.

Glacé Fruit Cake

Cake:
2-1/2 cups mixed glacé fruit, chopped
3/4 cup dried apricots, chopped
1 cup chopped pecans
Finely grated peel and juice 1 lemon
3 cups all-purpose flour
1 teaspoon baking powder
1-1/2 teaspoons ground mixed spice
1-2/3 cups ground almonds
1-3/4 cups superfine sugar
1-1/2 cups butter, softened
4 eggs

Topping:
1/4 cup apricot jam
2 teaspoons water
Mixed glacé fruit and nuts
Ribbon and holly sprigs to decorate

Preheat oven to 275F (135C). Line a 2-1/2-inch deep 8-inch-square cake pan or a 2-1/2-inch deep 9-inch-round pan with a double thickness of greased waxed paper, extending greased waxed paper above edge of pan. Place pan on baking sheet lined with a double thickness of waxed paper.

Combine glacé fruit, apricots, nuts and lemon peel and juice. Sift flour, baking powder and mixed spice into a bowl. Mix in ground almonds, sugar, butter and eggs, then beat 2 to 3 minutes or until smooth and glossy. Stir in mixed fruit and nuts.

Spoon mixture into prepared pan. Smooth top and bake 2-1/4 to 2-1/2 hours or until cake feels firm and springy. Cool in pan, then turn out and wrap in foil. In a saucepan, bring jam and water to a boil, stirring constantly, then sieve. Brush top of cake with jam. Arrange fruit and nuts over top and brush with remaining jam. Let stand until set. Decorate with ribbon and holly. Makes 30 servings.

Tiny Chocolate Logs

3 eggs
2 tablespoons plus 2 teaspoons superfine sugar
1/4 cup all-purpose flour
1 tablespoon cocoa powder
Powdered sugar, if desired
Marzipan toadstools and holly sprigs to
    decorate

Filling:
1-1/4 cups whipping cream
4 (1-oz.) squares semisweet chocolate

Preheat oven to 400F (205C). Line a 1-inch
deep 12-inch baking sheet with waxed paper.
Place eggs and sugar in a bowl set over a
saucepan of simmering water. Whisk until
thick and pale.

Remove bowl from saucepan; continue
whisking until mixture leaves a trail when
whisk is lifted. Sift flour and cocoa onto surface of mixture; fold in carefully until mixture is evenly blended. Pour mixture onto
prepared baking sheet; spread carefully to
edges. Bake in oven 8 to 10 minutes or until
firm to touch. Cool a few minutes and remove
cake. Remove waxed paper, trim edges and
cut cake in half. To prepare filling, place 1/4
cup whipping cream and chocolate broken
into pieces in a bowl set over saucepan of hot
water. Stir occasionally until melted. Whip
remaining cream until almost thick.

When chocolate has cooled, fold it carefully
into whipped cream. Using 1/3 of chocolate
cream, spread evenly over each cake. Roll
each in a firm roll from long edge. Wrap in
plastic wrap and chill 20 minutes or until
firm. Cut each roll in 6 lengths. Spread each
with remaining chocolate cream using a small
palette knife; mark cream in lines. Sprinkle
with powdered sugar, if desired. Decorate
with toadstools and holly. Refrigerate until
ready to serve. Makes 12 servings.

Chocolate Cigarettes

2 egg whites
1/3 cup plus 1 tablespoon superfine sugar
1/4 cup plus 3 tablespoons all-purpose flour
2 teaspoons cocoa powder
1/4 cup unsalted butter, melted
2 (1-oz.) squares white chocolate, melted
Holly sprigs to decorate

Preheat oven to 400F (205C). Line 2 baking sheets with waxed paper. In a bowl, whisk egg whites until stiff. Add sugar gradually, whisking well after each addition. Sift flour and cocoa over surface of mixture. Add butter and fold in carefully until mixture is evenly blended.

Place 2 spoonfuls of mixture onto each prepared baking sheet, spacing well apart. Spread each in a thin round. Bake 1 sheet at a time in oven 3 to 4 minutes. Loosen each round with a palette knife, then return to oven 1 minute.

Remove 1 chocolate round at a time and quickly roll around a greased pencil or wooden spoon handle to form a tube. Slip off and cool cigarette on a wire rack. Repeat with remaining rounds. Cook second tray of rounds, then repeat to make cigarettes. Dip both ends of each cigarette into melted chocolate. Let set on waxed paper-lined baking sheet. Store in an airtight container until needed. Decorate with holly sprigs. Makes 25 pieces.

Creme de Menthe Cookies

8 (1-oz.) squares semi-sweet chocolate
2 tablespoons butter
2 cups graham cracker crumbs
3/4 cup plain cake crumbs
Superfine sugar
Mint sprigs to decorate

Filling:
1/4 cup unsalted butter
3/4 cup powdered sugar, sieved
2 teaspoons Creme de Menthe

To prepare filling, beat butter in a bowl with a wooden spoon or electric mixer until soft and smooth. Gradually beat in powdered sugar and Creme de Menthe until light and fluffy.

Break up chocolate and place in a bowl with butter over a saucepan of hand-hot water. Stir occasionally until melted. Add graham cracker and cake crumbs; stir until evenly mixed and mixture forms a ball. Sprinkle a 10-inch square of foil with superfine sugar.

Roll out chocolate mixture on foil in an 8-inch square. Spread filling evenly over chocolate mixture to within 1/2 inch of edges. Roll up carefully from long edge in a smooth roll using foil. Wrap in foil and chill until firm. Cut in thin slices when needed. Decorate with mint sprigs. Makes 20 servings.

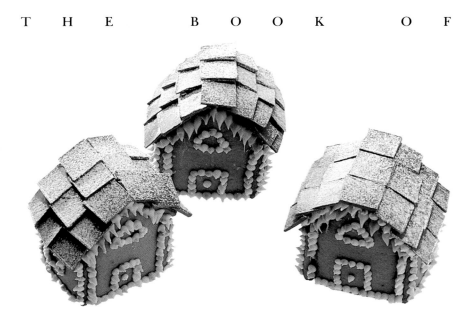

Gingerbread Houses

2 tablespoons light corn syrup
2 tablespoons molasses
2 tablespoons light-brown sugar
1/4 cup butter
1-1/2 cups all-purpose flour
1-1/2 teaspoons ground ginger
1/2 teaspoon baking soda
1 egg, beaten
4 (1-oz.) squares white chocolate
4 (1-oz.) squares semi-sweet chocolate
Pink, green and yellow food colorings
Powdered sugar

Preheat oven to 400F (205C). Line 2 baking sheets with waxed paper. In a saucepan, combine corn syrup, molasses, brown sugar and butter. Heat gently, stirring occasionally, until melted.

Sift flour and ginger into a bowl. Stir baking soda into melted mixture; add to flour with enough beaten egg to mix to form a soft dough. Knead on a lightly floured surface until smooth and free from cracks. Cut off 1/3 of dough and wrap in plastic wrap.

Roll out remaining 2/3 of dough thinly and cut out 32 (1-1/2-inch) squares of dough. Place spaced apart on a prepared baking sheet. Roll out remaining dough and cut out 16 (2-1/2- x 1-1/2-inches) rectangles. Measure and mark 1 inch down side of each rectangle. Cut from each mark to center of oblong to shape a "pitch" for "roof." Place on prepared baking sheet and bake in oven 8 to 10 minutes or until golden brown. Cool on a wire rack.

Break up and place white and dark chocolate into separate bowls over hand-hot water. Stir occasionally until melted. Divide white chocolate among 3 small bowls; color pink and green and yellow with food colorings. Assemble each house using semi-sweet chocolate to stick 2 side and 2 end walls together and 2 roof pieces in position. Let stand until set. Spread remaining chocolate over waxed paper.

When chocolate is almost set, invert onto piece of waxed paper. Peel off waxed paper and cut in 3/4-inch squares for roof tiles. Secure tiles onto roof with melted chocolate, starting at bottom of each roof and working to top. Fill 3 pastry bags with colored chocolate. Snip off points and pipe in doors, windows and colored beads of chocolate down all seams. Let stand until set. Dust with powdered sugar. Makes 8 houses.

Advent Cookies

1-1/4 cups all-purpose flour
1/3 cup butter
1/4 cup ground almonds
2 tablespoons plus 2 teaspoons superfine sugar
1 egg yolk
Cold water
1 egg white
1-1/2 cups powdered sugar, sifted
Red, green, yellow, and black food coloring
    pens
Assorted colors fine ribbon

Preheat oven to 350F (175C). Lightly flour 2 baking sheets. Sift flour into a bowl. Cut butter into flour finely until mixture resembles bread crumbs. Stir in ground almonds, sugar, egg yolk and enough cold water to form a soft dough.

Knead dough on a lightly floured surface. Roll out thinly and cut out 24 squares, rounds or ovals using a 2-1/4-inch cutter. Arrange on prepared baking sheet. Make a hole in top of each cookie with a drinking straw. Bake in oven 10 to 15 minutes or until lightly browned at edges. Cool on a wire rack.

In a bowl, combine egg white and enough powdered sugar to make a consistency of thick cream. Beat until smooth and glossy. Dip surface of each cookie into icing to cover evenly; allow excess to fall into bowl. Place on a rack to dry. When icing is dry and hard, use food coloring pens to number cookies 1 to 24 and draw a different design or message onto each cookie. Thread ribbons through holes at top and hang 1 up each day from December 1st to 24th. Makes 24 cookies.

Note:
Use remaining dough to make 1 special cookie for Christmas Day, if desired.

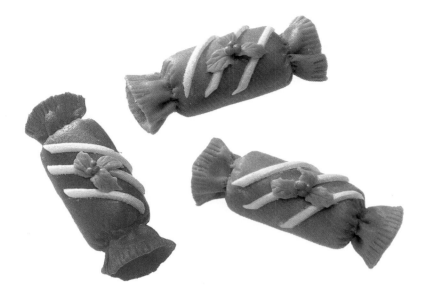

Christmas Treats

2 eggs
1/4 cup superfine sugar
1/2 cup all-purpose flour
Additional superfine sugar
1/2 cup apricot jam, boiled, and sieved
1 lb. white marzipan
Red, green and gold food colorings

Preheat oven to 375F (190C). Line bottom and sides of a 13" x 9" jelly roll pan with greased waxed paper. Place eggs and 1/4 cup sugar in a heatproof bowl over a saucepan of simmering water. Whisk mixture until thick and pale. Remove bowl from pan. Whisk until thick, cool and mixture leaves a trail when whisk is lifted.

Sift flour onto egg mixture. Fold in carefully using a spatula until all flour has been incorporated. Pour mixture into prepared pan. Bake in oven 10 to 15 minutes or until well risen and firm to touch. Sprinkle a piece of waxed paper with additional sugar. Invert cake, peel off paper and trim off edge with a large knife. Cut cake in half down length. Spread jam to within 1/2 inch of edges. Roll up each cake in 2 long thin rolls from long edges with help of paper. Cool on a wire rack, then cut in 12 mini-rolls. Brush mini-rolls with apricot jam.

Reserve 2 oz. of marzipan. Cut remainder in half. Color 1 piece red and 1 piece green with red and green food colorings. Roll out green marzipan thinly and cut out 6 (4-1/2" x 4") rectangles. Roll up 6 mini-rolls in marzipan with seam underneath. Squeeze ends together and flute. Repeat with red marzipan. Use trimmings to cut out holly leaves and berries from green and red marzipan. Roll out remaining marzipan and trim each with lattice strips. Brush with gold food coloring and decorate with holly and berries. Makes 12 pieces.

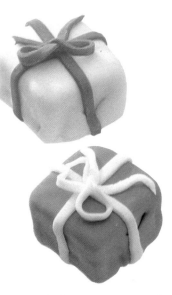

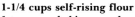

Christmas Gift Cakes

1-1/4 cups self-rising flour
1 teaspoon baking powder
1/3 cup hazelnuts, toasted, ground
3/4 cup superfine sugar
3/4 cup butter, softened
3 eggs
2 tablespoons apricot jam, boiled, sieved
1-1/4 lb. ready-to-roll fondant icing (sugar
    paste)
Red and green food colorings
Powdered sugar

Preheat oven to 325F (170C). Line bottom
and sides of a 2-1/2-inch deep 8-inch-square
cake pan with greased waxed paper. Sift flour
and baking powder into a bowl. Mix in hazelnuts, sugar, butter and eggs with a wooden
spoon. Beat 1 to 2 minutes or until smooth
and glossy. Spoon mixture into prepared
pan. Bake in oven 40 to 45 minutes or until
well risen and firm to touch in center. Cool in
pan 10 minutes. Remove cake, remove paper
and cool on a wire rack. When cake is completely cold, cut in 25 squares and brush each
with apricot jam.

Cut icing in 3 pieces. Color 2 pieces red and
green with food colorings. Cut a small piece
off each piece of icing and reserve for trim-
ming. Roll out white icing thinly on a lightly
sugared surface. Cut in 8 (2-inch) squares.

Cover 8 cakes with squares of white icing,
tucking excess icing under base of each cake.
Repeat with remaining icing and cakes,
covering 8 in red and 9 in green. Using reserved icing, roll out thin lengths and trim
each cake with "ribbons and bows." Let dry in
a warm place. Makes 25 cakes.

Maraschino Fruit Ring

1 cup self-rising flour
3/4 cup light-brown sugar
1/2 cup butter, softened
3 eggs
1/2 cup pecans, chopped
1/2 cup dark raisins
1/2 cup red maraschino cherries, drained,
    sliced
1/2 cup green glacé cherries, drained, sliced
1/2 cup powdered sugar, sifted
2 tablespoons plus 2 teaspoons maraschino
    cherry syrup
6 red and 6 green maraschino cherries, sliced
Holly sprig to decorate

Preheat oven to 300F (150C). Lightly oil a 9-inch ring mold. In a bowl, combine flour, brown sugar, butter and eggs until well mixed, then beat 1 to 2 minutes or until smooth and glossy. Add pecans, raisins and cherries to mixture; stir until evenly mixed. Spoon mixture into oiled ring mold. Level top and bake in oven about 1 hour or until cake feels firm to touch. Test with a skewer; when skewer is inserted into center of cake, skewer should come out clean. Loosen edges of cake with a knife and cool in pan. Invert onto a wire rack.

In a bowl, combine powdered sugar and enough cherry syrup to make a consistency of thick cream. Spoon icing over cold cake. Arrange cherry slices in clusters around top of cake. Let stand until set. Decorate with holly sprig. Makes 10 servings.

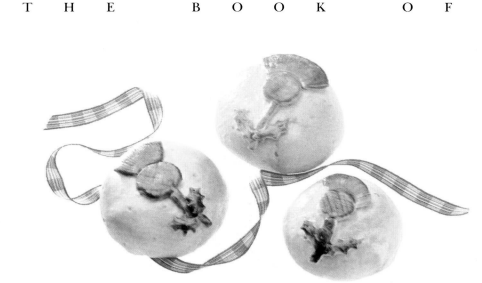

Scottish Black Buns

2 (6-oz.) pkgs. pizza crust mix
Warm water
1 egg yolk
1 teaspoon water
Purple and green food colorings

Filling:
1 cup mixed dried fruit
1/4 cup chopped glace cherries
1/4 cup chopped flaked almonds
Finely grated peel and juice 1 orange
2 tablespoons light-brown sugar
1/4 cup butter, melted
1/2 cup all-purpose flour
1 teaspoon ground allspice
1 egg, beaten

In a bowl, combine bread mix and warm water as directed on package. Knead 5 minutes. Place in a plastic bag and let stand until filling has been made. Preheat oven to 350F (175C). Lightly flour 2 baking sheets.

In a large bowl, combine dried fruit, cherries, almonds and orange peel and juice with a wooden spoon. Add brown sugar, butter, flour, allspice and egg; stir well until all ingredients are evenly mixed.

Knead dough on a lightly floured surface and cut in 11 pieces. Roll 1 piece at a time out thinly to a 5-inch round. Brush edge of round with water; place 1 heaping spoonful of filling in center of dough.

Draw up edge of dough to cover filling. Seal in center and shape in a smooth ball. Turn bun over with seam underneath. Place on prepared baking sheet. Repeat to make 9 more buns. Prick buns all over with a fine skewer.

Roll out remaining dough very thinly. Cut out 10 thistle shapes, stems and leaves. Brush each bun with 1 teaspoon of egg yolk mixed with water to glaze. Bake in oven 25 minutes and remove from oven.

Divide remaining egg yolk in half. Color 1 half purple and one half green with food colorings. Brush thistles purple and leaves and stems green 5 minutes before end of baking time to color evenly. Return to oven 5 minutes until glaze has set and buns are golden brown. Cool on a wire rack. Makes 10 buns.

Snowy Flip

4 eggs, separated
1/4 cup superfine sugar
1-1/4 cups whipping cream
2/3 cup milk, chilled
1 cup whiskey or brandy
Soda water
1 teaspoon ground mace
Orange and lemon peel to decorate

Place egg whites and egg yolks into separate bowls. Add 1/2 of sugar to yolks and whisk until pale and creamy. Wash beaters and whisk egg whites until stiff. Add remaining sugar and whisk until stiff.

Add egg whites to yolk mixture and fold in carefully until well mixed and foamy. In a bowl, whip cream until soft peaks form. Fold into egg mixture. Stir in milk and whisky or brandy. Cover with plastic wrap and chill until required.

Stir gently and divide cream mixture among 8 tall glasses. Fill up each with soda water and sprinkle with mace. Decorate with orange and lemon peel. Makes 8 servings.

Christmas Eve Mull

3-1/4 cups white wine
3-1/4 cups red wine
1-1/4 cups sweet red vermouth
1 tablespoon Angostura bitters
6 strips orange peel
8 whole cloves
1 cinnamon stick
8 cardamon pods, crushed
1 tablespoon dark raisins
1/2 cup superfine sugar
Lemon, orange and apple slices

Pour white and red wines into a large stainless steel or enamel saucepan.

Add vermouth, bitters, orange peel, cloves, cinnamon, and cardamon pods. Heat wine mixture gently until very hot but do not boil. Remove saucepan from heat, cover with a lid and cool. Strain wine into a bowl.

Just before serving, return wine to a clean saucepan. Add raisins and sugar. Heat gently until sugar has dissolved and wine is hot enough to drink. Add fruit slices and serve in heatproof mugs. Makes 16 servings.

Souchong Punch

1 Lapsang Souchong tea bag
2-1/2 cups boiling water
1 tablespoon plus 1 teaspoon light-brown sugar
1-1/4 cups clear apple juice
1/3 cup bourbon or brandy
2 lemon slices
3 lime slices
2-1/2 cups dry ginger ale
Ice cubes
Lemon geranium leaves

Place tea bag into a large glass measure. Pour in boiling water. Let tea infuse for 4 to 5 minutes without stirring, then remove tea bag. Stir in brown sugar and let stand until cold.

Add apple juice, bourbon or brandy and lemon and lime slices.

Just before serving, add ginger ale, ice cubes and lemon geranium leaves. Stir well and serve. Makes 12 servings.

Apples & Ale Mull

2 lb. cooking apples
5 cups ginger ale or ginger beer
6 whole cloves
1 blade mace
1 teaspoon grated nutmeg
1/2 teaspoon ground ginger
3 strips orange peel
Red and green apple and lemon slices

Preheat oven to 400F (205C). Wash apples and remove stalks. Arrange on a baking sheet and bake in oven 30 to 40 minutes or until soft.

Place apples in a saucepan and mash to break up apples. Add ginger ale or ginger beer, cloves, mace, ginger and orange peel. Bring to a boil. Remove from heat and cool. Strain apple mixture through a nylon sieve into a bowl, pressing through as much apple as possible.

Just before serving, return apple and ale mixture to a clean saucepan. Heat until hot enough to drink. Float apple and lemon slices on top and serve in heatproof glasses or mugs. Makes 10 servings.

Hot Buttered Rum

4 sticks cinnamon
1 tablespoon plus 1 teaspoon light-brown sugar
1/2 cup dark rum
2-2/3 cups apple cider
2 tablespoons butter
1 teaspoon ground mace
4 lemon slices

Evenly divide cinnamon sticks, brown sugar and rum among 4 warm heatproof glasses or mugs.

In a saucepan, heat apple cider until very hot but not boiling. Fill each glass or mug to top with apple cider.

Add a dot of butter to each. Sprinkle with mace and add a lemon slice. Stir well and serve. Makes 4 servings.

Rosé Glow

1/4 cup sweet red vermouth
1/4 cup cherry brandy liqueur
1/4 cup brandy
1 kiwifruit, peeled, sliced
8 maraschino cherries, halved
Orange, lemon and lime slices
1 bottle rosé wine
Ice cubes
Mint and borage sprigs
Rose petals, if desired
1 bottle sparkling white wine

In a large punch bowl, pour vermouth, cherry brandy and brandy. Add kiwifruit, cherries and citrus fruit slices. Stir to mix well.

Just before serving, pour in rosé wine. Add ice cubes, mint and borage sprigs and rose petals, if desired.

At the last minute, add sparkling wine and serve in punch glasses or cups, including some fruit and ice. Makes 10 servings.

Snowball Fizz

4 (1-oz.) squares white chocolate
Finely grated peel and juice 2 limes
1-1/2 cups red or white grape juice
1 egg white
1 tablespoon plus 2 teaspoons superfine sugar
Soda or sparkling water
1 teaspoon grated milk chocolate
4 drinking straws
4 cocktail umbrellas, if desired

Break up white chocolate. Place in bowl set over a saucepan of hand-hot water. Stir occasionally until melted and smooth. Stir in lime peel and juice until well blended.

Divide grape juice equally among 4 glasses. Add 1/4 of chocolate-lime mixture to each and stir until well blended.

In a bowl, whisk egg white until stiff. Add sugar a little at a time and whisk until thick. Just before serving, divide meringue among glasses and fill to top with soda or sparkling water. Sprinkle with milk chocolate and serve with drinking straws and cocktail umbrellas, if desired. Makes 4 servings.

Sunrise & Sunset

1/3 cup apricot nectar juice
1/3 cup pineapple juice
2/3 cup lemonade
2/3 cup sparkling orange juice
1 tablespoon plus 1 teaspoon grenadine syrup
Ice cubes
2 lemon slices
2 drinking straws

Using 2 goblets or tumblers, pour apricot nectar into 1 glass and pineapple juice in other glass. Add lemonade to apricot juice and sparkling orange juice to pineapple juice.

Carefully spoon 2 teaspoons of grenadine syrup into each drink; allow it to settle at bottom of each glass.

Add ice cubes and lemon slices and serve with a drinking straw. Makes 2 servings.

Decorative Bread Rings

2 cups all-purpose flour, sifted
1/2 teaspoon superfine sugar
1/2 teaspoon salt
1 tablespoon butter
1 teaspoon active dry yeast
1/2 cup warm water
1 egg yolk
1 teaspoon water
Red and green food coloring, if desired
Colored ribbon

In a bowl, combine sifted flour, sugar and salt. Cut butter into flour mixture finely. Stir in yeast and enough warm water to form a soft dough. Knead on a lightly floured surface until smooth and no longer sticky or use a food processor fitted with a plastic blade.

Return dough to bowl. Cover with plastic wrap and let stand 5 minutes. Re-knead dough until smooth. Cut off 1/4 of dough and reserve. Shape remainder in a 24-inch roll. Cut roll in half. Shape in rings by joining ends together. Seal with water and place on a floured baking sheet. Cover and let stand in a warm place to rise 20 to 30 minutes. Meanwhile, roll out remaining dough very thinly. Using a holly cutter, cut out about 40 holly leaves and mark veins with a knife. Shape 40 beads of dough for berries. Arrange on a floured plate. Cover with plastic wrap and place in a cool place. Preheat oven to 425F (220C).

Divide egg yolk among 3 egg cups. Add water to 1 and brush dough rings to glaze. Add green food coloring to 1 and red to other cup. Bake dough rings 10 to 15 minutes or until risen but pale in color. Remove rings from oven. Arrange holly leaves and berries on rings. Glaze leaves green and berries red and return rings to oven 5 to 6 minutes until glaze has set. Cool on a wire rack. Tie with ribbon to use as decorations or serve as bread. Makes 2 rings.

Chocolate Decorations

4 (1-oz.) squares semi-sweet chocolate
8 (1-oz.) squares white chocolate
Pink, green and yellow oil-based or powdered
    food colorings
Pink, green and yellow fine ribbon

Break up each chocolate and place in separate bowls set over saucepans of hand-hot
water. Stir occasionally until melted. Divide
1/2 of white chocolate into 3 bowls. Color each
pink, green and yellow with food colorings.

Draw around novelty cookie cutters on parchment paper. Half-fill 2 small pastry bags with
dark chocolate. Snip a small point off 1 bag
and pipe a fine outline of chocolate following
shapes. Fill center of each shape with remaining dark chocolate, snipping a larger point off
end so that shapes look over-filled and
rounded.

Repeat to make different shaped chocolate
decorations, using white and some colored
chocolate as above. Let stand until hard.
Carefully peel off paper, taking care not to
mark surface. Sandwich matching shapes
together with melted chocolate, placing ribbon loops in between. Decorate shapes with
piped colored chocolate using a small pastry
bag with end snipped off. Pipe lines, dots,
zig-zags, lattice or write Christmas messages.
Allow all decorations to dry before hanging
up with ribbons. Makes about 20 decorations.

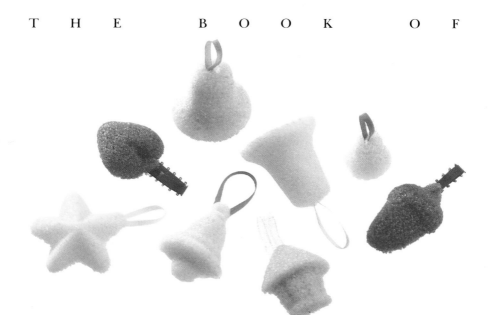

Sugar-Crystal Decorations

1-3/4 cups superfine sugar
3 to 4 teaspoons cold water
Blue, pink, green and yellow food colorings
Colored fine ribbons

Place sugar in a bowl. Add a little cold water at a time, stirring with a fork, until sugar is like damp sand. Divide sugar among 5 bowls. Leave 1 white and tint remaining 4 pale blue, pink, green and yellow.

Using plastic Christmas decoration mold shapes or figures, fill 1 shape at a time and press firmly to pack well. To insert ribbon for hanging decorations, place a loop of ribbon when mold is only half-filled, then fill to top and press down well. Or make a hole with a skewer when sugar has almost set. Repeat filling molds with colored sugar. Place a flat tray over top of molds and invert. Lift off molds and leave sugar shapes to dry in a warm place.

Fill larger molds like bells, cones or half egg shells with sugar and pack well. Invert on a tray. Let stand until sugar has set forming a crust. Return shape to mold. Scoop out sugar from center leaving a hollow shape. Make holes for ribbons with skewer. Remove from molds and let dry. Thread ribbons through to hang sugar decorations. Try decorating or painting using a fine paint brush and food colorings or food coloring pens. Makes about 25 decorations.

Sugar Christmas Card

1 teaspoon plain gelatin
1 tablespoon cold water
1 teaspoon liquid glucose
1 teaspoon shortening
1-1/2 cups powdered sugar, sifted
1/2 teaspoon gum tragacanth
1/2 egg white
Green and red food colorings
Powdered sugar icing
Assorted colors food coloring pens
Assorted colors fine ribbon

Sprinkle gelatin over cold water and soften 2 to 3 minutes. Stand bowl in a saucepan of hot water and stir until dissolved and hot. Add liquid glucose and shortening; stir until melted. Combine powdered sugar, gum tragacanth, egg white and gelatin mixture to form a soft paste.

Knead on a surface lightly dusted with powdered sugar until sugar paste is white and smooth. Keep sealed in a plastic bag until needed. Thinly roll out about 1/3 of sugar paste and cut out 2 (3-inch) squares. Flute or scallop edges on 3 sides of both pieces using a small cutter or icing crimper. Using a tiny round cutter or end of a pastry nozzle, cut out small rounds in between scalloped edges. Cut 2 large holes down side of plain edge evenly spaced apart from center with small cutter on both pieces. Dry on a flat surface sprinkled with cornstarch .

Color trimmings with red and green food colorings. Make tiny berries from red icing. Roll and cut out holly leaves from green icing. Mark veins with a knife and let dry. Thread ribbon in and out of the holes around edges. Attach holly leaves and berries on front of card with powdered sugar icing. Draw a design with food coloring pens and write a message on inside of card. Tie 2 pieces of card together with ribbon to join card. Makes about 6 cards.

INDEX